The Author

Vivian Linacre's commercial property career extends over 60 years, working in agency and development in England and Scotland. He was a Founding Member of the British Council of Shopping Centres and also of the Society of Property Researchers.

Member of the Management Committee of the International Real Estate Federation's British Chapter from 1976-83 and a regular contributor to professional journals.

Founder of SPIFOX, (*Scottish Property Industry Festival of Christmas*) the children's charity wholly supported by the Scottish property professions & building industry, which continues to grow.

Chairman of the Scottish Appeal Committee for the United Nations 1987 Year of Shelter for the Homeless.

Chairman of the British Weights & Measures Association from 1995 until elected President in 2003 and now a Trustee.

Also by Vivian Linacre

Megalithic Measures and Rhythms (with Richard A Batchelor) (Floris Books, 2006) ISBN 0-86315-554-5

The General Rule - A Guide to Customary Weights and Measures (The Squeeze Press, 2007) ISBN 978-906069-01-8

The Marshall Place Conspiracy (2008) ISBN 978-0-9560082-0-6

A New Lease of Life (Conservative Political Centre, 1975) ISBN 0 85070 575 4

GROUND-BREAKING

How the commercial property market got off the ground

1950-1975

VIVIAN LINACRE

Ground-Breaking

Edited by Nigel Linacre
Cover design by Cordelia Linacre
ISBN 10: 095561502X
ISBN 13: 9780955615023

Contents

1 ANTECEDENTS

This is a chronicle of the commercial property market in Britain from its beginnings around 1950, when post-war recovery at last got under way. No commercial property market had existed in any economic sense before that date – which also coincided with the start of my working life.

Throughout the history of civilization in every country, a market had always flourished in land, as a store of wealth and an index of status. For over a thousand years a market in farms and estates contended with military and religious conflict as well as with dynastic influences. By the 18th century the industrial revolution in Britain obliged owners of coal-mines, steel-works, factories and shipyards to provide housing on a vast scale for their labour, establishing a popular market in rented housing that soon extended to the opposite end of the social scale for the new merchant class and urban gentry. But a market in shops and offices had to wait for the post-1945 politico-economic revolution that generated a property-owning democracy and a consumerist society.

Perhaps the single most important reason, however, why a commercial property market could not be conceived until after the War was because, while overwhelming public need might be described as the market's mother, its father had to be the investment of institutional funds; but such prime sources had no market of their own – a pre-requisite of going into circulation for trading in any sector of an embryonic property market. Then suddenly this nebulous market in institutional property investment split.

On the one hand was the insurance industry, highly respected in the real estate world though ultra-conservative and largely in suspense during the War, but boomed once normal life was restored, and soon took the lead in this new commercial property sector, which provided an ideal fresh outlet in physical form, functional and geographical spread, size of lots, ease of management and prospects for real growth. On the other hand was the infant pensions industry, which until after the War was largely confined to the civil service and non-manual classes of industry, but was transformed by the creation of the welfare state, nationalisation of heavy industries and explosive growth in bureaucracy at every level. That placed enormous power into the hands of trade unions as well as the socialist government, who enforced introduction of pension schemes, which spread to mega-companies in the private sector and thence universally.

These twin towers of institutional investment accumulated vast sums in insurance premiums and pension contributions, for which commercial property investment presented such a perfect medium. Investment led to development which led to equity participation, to beat competition from the banks, which then tried to catch up quickly, with dire results. The interesting question is whether it was the case that economic, political and social conditions were so favourable that the emergence of this new sector was inevitable and was merely facilitated by these new funding sources, or whether this process was to a greater or lesser extent actually driven by the weight of this new money and the need to find it a good home. In either event, the compelling incentive to invest long-term in commercial property was that it afforded as solid as possible a proof against inflation, the factor which came to dominate the British economy from the 1960s onwards. The statistics are familiar, but as good an index as any is the value of farm land with vacant possession in England & Wales, which in 1950 averaged £80 per acre and rose to £288 in 1973, falling suddenly to £144 in 1975, then recovering and soaring almost continually ever since.

But until long-term funds became available, finance always had to be improvised. A few spectacular commercial developments had indeed been completed before the War – e.g. Costain's Dolphin Square, A J Phillips' Broadcasting House, Harold Colebrook's Burlington Arcade, Charles Clore's Prince of Wales Theatre, Jack Cotton's early schemes in Birmingham – but funding was always *ad hoc*. Obtaining a building licence was much easier, and so was bank lending, for "lessor "projects – i.e. when pre-let to any of the scores of government departments or public bodies that were avid for space – of which the grand-daddy was surely Emmanuel Curtis' 1947 Adastral House on Theobalds Road: all 300,000 sq.ft. let to the Air Ministry on a 63 years lease at a fixed rent! (And it was a great-nephew of his, Sefton Myers, who pioneered decentralised office development in 1960 with Yeoman House at Kew Bridge.)

Conditions by the early 1950s were almost ideal. Sterling had devalued in 1949. Capital gains were tax-free. The 1953 Town and Country Planning Act abolished the development charge system and building licences were abolished in 1954 – the year of the great Landlord & Tenant Act. It was in 1953, too, that Charles Clore acquired True-Form, revolutionising both the technique of the takeover bid and also the occupational lease-back, *of which more later.* Until 1957 there was no separate "Property" Section in the lists of quoted companies: they were scattered among 'Miscellaneous Industries' and 'Financial Trusts'. There were only 35 quoted property companies in 1939, growing to 111 in 1957 and 163 in 1968. Bank Rate in 1952 was 4% and the trend was downward. It was Alec Colman who hailed "Those ten glorious years -- 1952 to 1962!" By 1952 the assets of Land Securities Investment Trust amounted to some £11m, the company having been bought by Harold Samuel in 1944, when the previous annual report disclosed that all it owned was three houses in Kensington Court (two were unoccupied) and government securities worth less than £20,000; yet by 1968 the assets had increased to £204m.

But in 1955, after only three good years, a credit squeeze was imposed; so new techniques had to be devised to overcome the restrictions imposed by the Credit Control Committee and enforced by the banks. At that time there was not a single link between a property company and a funding institution which provided for both equity participation and development finance; so there were no buyers when Church Commissioners put the Paddington Estate on the market until Max Rayne produced a formula whereby he took a building lease to carry out the development in partnership with the freeholders – a solution which soon became standard practice. Equity sharing with major contractors likewise became fashionable – e.g. Stock Conversion with George Wimpey – as did joint companies between a developer and a life office such as Charles Clore with the Legal & General.

Institutions were becoming increasingly keen to provide development finance because of the sheer growth of their disposable income; investment in this sector by such funds having already doubled between 1945 and 1953. Earnings yields, the actual return from first-class commercial developments on completion, still exceeded lending rates, but no real growth was possible if leases (both head and sub) were granted for long periods at rents that were fixed throughout. So it was the adoption of rent reviews that finally won the institutions over to this sector of the new market: initially at 33 year intervals in 99 years leases for commercial premises and at 21 years in 42 or 63 year leases for industrials; shrinking rapidly ever since.

The next refinement was a stake in the equity in addition to rent reviews, and a very large stake if the developer's object was bridging as well as permanent finance. Then came gearing the headlease rent to the rack-rent rises; and hence every variety of option and partnership. The boom resumed after the credit squeeze was lifted in 1958, until the recession of 1962-63, resuming once more thereafter for another "ten glorious years" (interrupted only by a few brief, mild depressions) until the great crash at the end of 1973. By then, in terms of economic history, we had a mature market, tried and tested. But if the name of the game until 1973 was greed, from 1974 onwards it was fear: a cycle repeated so precisely thirty-five years later!

The commercial property sector is like a faded pop star, whose infancy coincided with the economic recovery of the early 1950s, whose parents were the construction industry and estate agency, whose godparents were the new town-planning legislation, which provided a framework for demand, and the investment institutions which were straining against the gilt-edged straitjacket. The child was vigorous and imaginative or willful and destructive, depending on one's point of view but endured a painful adolescence before emerging into a riotous early manhood. It celebrated its coming-of-age in 1971 with the Green Paper on 'Competition and Credit Control' when fame and fortune went to its head and a rake's progress led to gambling debts and drugs which threatened ruin. But after a period of austerity and rehabilitation it discovered a new respectability – until, as we are all too well aware, the second time round!

The Centre for Advanced Land Use Studies held two conferences under the title "Investment in Property"; one in 1971 under the chairmanship of Edward Du Cann, a very senior Conservative statesman and chairman of Keyser Ullmann, and the other in 1974 presided over by the then managing director of Slater Walker Investments, each of whom presented to his august assembly a sublimely hubristic review of the subject, blissfully oblivious to the catastrophe that was about to overtake them, which rendered their papers worthless even before publication.

A fundamental difference between the two crashes is that the major casualties in 1973-4 were individuals – recklessly over-exposed -- whereas in 2008-9 they were companies, because meanwhile the tycoons had learnt how to protect themselves. Britain's biggest-ever bankrupt was William Stern, a Harvard graduate who, when joining his father-in-law with the Freshwater Group around 1960, had no experience whatever of UK law, property or business practice, yet soon set up on his own and built a colossal property empire, blithely signing personal guarantees for more than £100 million (over a billion today), so that when all was lost he ruined scores of innocent professionals and tenants too.

The other archetypal property tycoon was Ronald Lyon (just four months older than me) who went bust no fewer than four times between 1954 and 1983, yet was starting all over again a few years before he died in 2004. Starting as a boy at home building garden sheds to sell at £16.10s apiece, he became Britain's biggest developer of industrial estates, boasting that before he went spectacularly bust in 1974 his group had let a new unit every week since 1958. British industry – what hadn't been devastated by the blitz – was largely housed in obsolete premises, so Lyon applied new fabrication techniques for assembly of large flexible structures as well as buying cheap war-surplus properties for rapid refurbishment and leasing. It is easy to blame the excesses of the property industry for that first great crash (just as it is easy to blame the banks for this second one), but actually the outgoing Conservative government's high interest rates, panic freeze on rents and introduction of development land tax – all so predictably counter-productive – were major contributory factors. Lyon's company was still private, with just £3 million of capital supporting £93 million of debt from 35 banks.

His creditors sold everything, including the £3 million 188ft long 650 ton yacht which he had commissioned but never sailed. But neither the glamour of his imperious heyday nor the long sequel of slapdash enterprises should obscure his importance as the pioneer of industrial estate development and the last of the all-round buccaneers.

So yes, it is a history, but a history narrated at first hand from my direct experience. It covers the period which neatly fits into the third quarter of the last century, extending from the birth of the commercial property market through its evolution, up to the property crash of the mid-70s, by which time both the market and my parallel career had reached some kind of maturity.

The creation of a national market-place in shop and office property and development sites, broadly indicating universally recognized rental values and investment yields according to precise location, layout and condition – approximately enough for professionals to debate and negotiate around – also required such essential elements as a stable planning regime (Town and Country Planning Act 1947) and a far-sighted legislative framework (Landlord and Tenant Act 1954) as well as freedom from building controls (abolition of war-time restrictions again in 1954). So the beginning of this narrative marks the very origin of the subject itself.

After its 'Big Bang' in the early 1950s, this market grew at such a phenomenal rate because explosive pent-up demand was released by entrepreneurism of a generation of adventurous developers in a post-war spirit of Utopian emancipation and harnessed to the professionalism of a few firms of far-sighted agents. The surveying and valuation skills, of course, were always there – sustained by long traditions in building and agriculture, in acting for trusts and in management of rented housing and estates – ready for application to these novel commercial commodities.

I finish then, after that explosive quarter-century, in the midst of the first slump, which was so like what we are suffering now in the midst of the second, despite the vast changes that occurred during the intervening 30-odd years. One main difference between the two is that today we do at least know exactly what had caused it, whereas a generation ago we had no idea what was going on (beyond a trebling of oil and world food prices) and virtually no means of discovering why it had happened.

Yet the causes even of the present slump have been identified and analyzed only in retrospect, as almost nobody had seen it coming, despite the huge advantages enjoyed by our contemporary commentators of greater transparency, electronic media and information technology, a closely monitored monetary regime, institutional and professional research departments – plus, of course, the enormous benefit of *déjà vu*! Sub-prime mortgages were as mysterious in 2008 as secondary banking had been in 1973. All that the respective causes of the successive disasters apparently had in common was decades of national and domestic profligacy.

That period from Churchill's final premiership, on the expiry of the post-war Socialist government in 1951 to the replacement of Edward Heath's administration by another Labour regime in 1975 – from the disintegration of the British Empire to the emergence of the European Economic Community – witnessed social, cultural and industrial revolutions which enormously influenced the creation of a market in our sector. Ought we not, therefore, to have more thoroughly examined and absorbed their implications, as well as the lessons of the minor recessions of the early '80s and 90s; long before the unsustainable boom that led inevitably yet blindly to the current crisis?

Oliver Marriott wrote in his book 'The Property Boom' (Hamilton 1967): "The era of the property tycoon as the arch-symbol of capitalism is over. Forces of competition and taxation have ended the days when an individual could rapidly amass a fortune with a few well-chosen deals or developments." Yet, as he could never have foreseen, that was just when the biggest ever property boom was about to explode, largely driven by a few dozen brilliant egos. Nor could he have dreamt that, thirty years later, an even bigger boom would make many individuals spectacular fortunes.

There are still millionaires created by a few blocks of ultra-expensive apartments in the West End or the odd skyscraper office-development in the city, for which it is unnecessary ever to venture outside London or learn much about the property business but merely to exploit freaks of demand; so they will not be remembered in any sequel to this book – though nobody should begrudge the vast rewards that such finely tuned judgement of market trends and monumental courage can bring. The likelihood of limited life-expectancy of structure and services in buildings designed to cater for such ephemeral market niches is not their problem.

The editorial article in 'The Estates Gazette' of 6 December 1969 wrote: "So short is the time-scale of change that circumstances can alter radically while plans are put into operation....The population explosion came as a complete surprise to the government planners – indeed the statistics had fore-shadowed a diminishing population....Today planners are undoubtedly preparing for a vast increase in our population."

But though long-range forecasting is impossible, the industry's roots which grew during that first quarter-century are still spreading and strengthening. To analyze those roots is the purpose of this book. Only by recognizing how much has the commercial property market achieved from zero only sixty-odd years ago can one also recognize its infinite future potential, for the benefit of the economy and society. Certainly, the industry has proved highly successful, popular and efficient.

It amply fulfils highly volatile public demands through violently changing economic and social conditions, within unpredictable political constraints. Yet it is wholly initiated, financed, undertaken, directed, implemented and managed by private enterprise. In contrast, the housing sector, although catering for a universal need and presenting no inherent difficulties, is subject to continuous doctrinaire and bureaucratic interference, direction and regulation, yet has always been a total disaster! Is there a moral somewhere?

I do not claim to have produced a significant work of academic research, except in the Proustian sense of *'A La Récherche du Temps Perdu'*. My motivation has always been to search rather than to research! There are no computer-generated spreadsheets, graphs or tables. Everything worth learning from the past was new in its time: now we must pioneer the future rather than attempt to plot it. Besides, a cardinal principle of research is impartiality, to which this account cannot pretend since it is confined to my own records, reminiscence, anecdote and speculation.

Nevertheless, while my personal life is irrelevant, I must quickly explain how I reached that starting-point some sixty years ago. After national service and Edinburgh University (History and English – a joy but not much practical use), I went to work on a modern dairy-farm in the Scottish Borders with a view to studying in my spare time for an external BSc. degree in Estate Management by correspondence with the College of Estate Management, which was then in St Albans Grove, Kensington. The owner let me spend evenings studying in his office in the big house and even helped with the cost of attending the Cambridge University Estate Management Club summer school at Trinity Hall in 1952.

That, by the way, was then one of the very few universities offering full-time degree courses in estate management ('land economy') as distinct from agriculture; otherwise gaining qualifications was by evening classes or correspondence courses while learning on the job. So when my mother and brother wanted to settle in London, I decided to go with them and secure employment there, switching from rural to urban practice, with the deferred intention of sitting intermediate exams in 1954.

If only I had known then that there was such a chronic shortage of educated young men in the capital city in that post-war period, I could have walked in almost anywhere. But I felt sure that a very small firm of general practitioners would be best where I could start at the bottom, anywhere in the heart of the Estates Agents' quarter in Mayfair (bounded by Hanover, Grosvenor and Berkeley Squares) where I could become thoroughly acclimatized.

So, in the village shop near the farm I bought the 'Daily Telegraph' (apart from specialist journals the market for professional appointments before the emergence of recruitment agencies operated via "situations vacant" columns in the national dailies) and there it was! I telephoned, got an interview, took the overnight bus to London from Edinburgh costing £1.50 return, from an ordinary bus stop on Queen Street (long, slow journey – no motorways), was offered the job; bus back next night, confirmatory letter arrived the following day and a fortnight later we headed South.

2 APPRENTICE

There never was a Mr Way in Way & Waller at 7 Hanover Square – a house in the middle of the East side, which was redeveloped in the 1970s. As senior partner, effectively the proprietor, Sam Waller felt the combination sounded more impressive and easier to remember: "Where there's a Waller there's a Way". He had started with one room on an upper floor in Clifford Street off Bond Street, with a clerk, Sid Baines, who soldiered on to become my first colleague. He recalled that adjacent to that single room was a lavatory, on the door of which Sam Waller had fixed a sign, "General Office"; so that whenever footsteps were heard on the stairs Sid would disappear with a typewriter perched on his lap, clattering loudly, to give the impression of busy staff. The only other partners were Sam Waller's close friends, Mr Arnold (valuations) and Mr Simmons (investments), who collectively initiated me into the post-war world of commercial real estate.

One of the other two departments was town & country houses, headed by professional associates under Major Collingwood-Caird (who later joined J Trevor & sons who later amalgamated with Webster & Co of Glasgow before they merged with Conrad Ritblat who eventually became part of Colliers world-wide) plus an invaluable socialite as roving ambassador, Dudley Delevigne, whose elite contacts brought in top-class business. His most spectacular coup that I recall, causing much excitement in the office, was the sale of a great Tudor house, Sutton Place near Guildford, on behalf of the Duke of Rutland to Jean Paul Getty, ranked by *'Fortune'* magazine in 1957 as the richest living American. (It is owned today by the richest man in Britain, the Russian oligarch Alisher Usmanov.)

But the most exciting day of all was witnessing, as we crowded around the front door, Leonid Brezhnev and Nikita Khrushchev passing through Hanover Square on their visit for meetings with Anthony Eden's government during the 1956 Suez crisis.

The other department, where I worked, specialized in hotels, restaurants, going concerns (mainly cafes, newsagents, confectioners & tobacconists) and apartment houses – what were known then as flatlet houses, i.e. bedsitting rooms equipped with a sink and a one-ring cooker, usually a Bellings. After thirteen years of food rationing and travel restrictions there was a desperate shortage of hotels, and because of war-damage and the still widespread prevalence of long leasehold tenure there was not much of a mortgageable house-purchase market for the middle classes. No new blocks of flats had been built, while the punitive Rent Restriction Acts had eliminated unfurnished accommodation for letting.

So investors had to exempt their premises by not merely furnishing but also providing nominal catering facilities. Consequently, tens of thousands of office workers and other single people and couples, young and old, were crammed into these cells, ten or twenty of which were formed out of each of vast numbers of Georgian and Victorian houses. They were chiefly concentrated in west central London, from Hampstead to Harlesden to Hammersmith, although extending round to Highbury and Stoke Newington. Almost all, of course, were dilapidated after war-time neglect.

The biggest concentration were around Paddington – except that in estate agents' parlance Paddington did not exist, because of its unsavoury reputation, so the address given was the closest to which the property could stretch: Marble Arch, Hyde Park, Maida Vale or, at worst, Bayswater. (The most fashionable districts today, the twin poles of Notting Hill and Islington, were then very run down, even slummy.) Every one of those houses would be closed today for wholesale violations of Health & Safety regulations. Any inspection for purpose of a sale always looked especially for fire hazards or signs of vermin or other infestation, and many inspections failed because the vendor could not produce a fire certificate or an adequate insurance policy, if any.

We sold young Max Joseph (later Sir Maxwell, died 1982) his first hotel, Flemings in Half-Moon Street, together with the adjacent Manetta's Restaurant. He had been an army corporal stationed at Uxbridge towards the end of the war, and spent his short spells of leave exploring bomb-damaged properties which could be acquired and (using compensation grants) restored for conversion into flatlet houses; but my departmental head foresaw the inevitable boom in hotels so persuaded him to diversify into what – apart, of course, from the bookmaker Ladbroke's – became his main activity, building first the Grand Metropolitan and thence the Norfolk Capital Group. To Max Joseph, as he put it to me, a hotelier was simply in the business of letting space at a hefty premium; a definition which would horrify any professional hotelier! That conversation took place by candle-light at Hotelympia, the trade show where Way & Waller took a stand, during which the electricians' trade union staged a 'lightning' strike.

The firm was severely reprimanded by the professional estate agency bodies – the Incorporated Society of Auctioneers & Landed Property Agents,

Royal Institution of Chartered Surveyors and Chartered Auctioneers & Estate Agents Institute – for exhibiting at a trade show, in breach of the regulations which severely restricted advertising. Today, when every firm of estate agents and surveyors, as well as the hallowed professions of the law and accountancy, are necessarily engaged in marketing and promotional activities – the biggest of them even producing merchandise and sponsoring sporting events – such advertising prohibitions seem incredible. They derived solely from snobbery, the pretence that we were gentlemen and had nothing to do with trade or anything so vulgar as "crying one's wares". So that was Way & Waller's first and last exhibition.

I learnt a great deal from the astuteness and flamboyance of this newly emerging class of property tycoons. I also learnt that scarcely a soul in that world, client or agent, had any financial conscience. The chief attraction of the business of 'flatlets' (as they were known then, a term long since displaced by the all-purpose 'apartments'), of course, was that it was largely cash. Tenants who paid by cheque and/or needed receipts to show their employers, were tolerated but not encouraged – and were charged slightly more: those were the transactions which duly appeared in the accounts. So typically, 4 guineas a week by cheque, while the majority paid 3 guineas in cash but 2 guineas according to the accounts. The shilling-in-the-slot gas meters, to which the supply was adjustable, also provided a useful supplementary income. So did any discretionary additional services such as laundry, wines, and use of the telephone. Few houses, however large, had more than one telephone, if any, as eighteen months on the waiting-list preceded installation for domestic use, though Mr Waller's connections got me SHE2636 within a fortnight. (The GPO monopoly, which continued until privatization in the 1980s, laid itself open to such abuses.)

All this meant that, in producing a valuation to agree an asking price, I had to take account of the huge discrepancy between declared revenue for tax purposes and my estimate of actual takings: i.e. calculating the declared ('base') figure plus the 'equity' – but I had to do so tacitly, without disclosing the process. Conversely, when negotiating with a prospective buyer, I had to hint that there were two sets of books but only the official one could be revealed, from which it was up to the interested party to project the other.

Equally disillusioning was the discovery that at the top end of the restaurant trade the priority was presentation, not so much of the dishes – which were not worth writing about – as of the establishment itself. Fifty-odd years ago, the gentry and business people still frequented night-clubs, every high-class restaurant catered for dancing or at least provided a band and a vocalist or two, but my abiding memory of them all is the premises' sleazy state in the cold light of early morning when I had to conduct my inspections, without the glamorous lighting and tinsel. So the presentation of accounts was just another game of smoke and mirrors – and it seemed that the more august the name the more illusory their financial statements. Post-War life in general then was like that; wearing a heavily made-up face to conceal the impoverished reality, the 'spivs' and racketeers, and the daunting scale of recovery that lay ahead.

It was not until 1950 that sugar, eggs and soap "came off the ration"; and petrol too, when there were fewer than three million motorists and a doubling in tax had raised the price to 3s/-d a gallon. The 1951 census revealed that almost 40% of the nation's entire housing stock had been built before 1891; half of that before 1851. It also revealed that 50.8% of Glasgow's homes comprised only one or two rooms compared to 5.5% for Greater London; and that Glasgow's residential density was 163 persons per acre compared to 48 for Birmingham and 77 for Manchester – yet even in those English cities over-crowding and inadequate sanitation were recognized as intolerable.

Between 1945 and 1951, a *total* of 807,000 dwellings were built for local authorities and a pitiful 180,000 in the private sector. Our lives were governed by the State. It was effectively a liberal soviet economy, requiring licences and permits for almost everything. But the British don't complain, merely grumble, War-time regimentation having become ingrained.

After the ruling Labour administration's setback in the 1950 general election, a Gallup Poll that autumn demonstrated the electorate's disappointment with the performance of such nationalised industries as gas and electricity, railways and road transport, and a consequent lack of support for the government's commitment to nationalise the steel industry as well as insurance, sugar, cement, chemicals and cement. So not surprisingly it was swept out of office the following year, ending several years of frustration and inertia.

Until thereafter, no market in commercial property could possibly have existed. Improvisation *ad hoc* prevailed. Not even a statutory framework for the operation of a market existed until the great Landlord & Tenant Act of 1954, supported by the Town & Country Planning legislation of 1947, 53 & 54, on all which I was weaned. Building controls were at last ended in November

54, enabling a private house-building industry to get under way, and pioneering entrepreneurs in town centre development to start prowling in the Home Counties.

In 1953, when Gina Lollobrigida opened the first Moka coffee bar in Frith Street, with its gleaming Gaggia espresso machine, and Wimbledon heralded the debut of the Wimpy beefburger ("the meal in a bun"), the masses were awestruck as if by visitations from another planet. Food rationing did not end finally until midnight on 3rd July 1954. Television advertising began in September 1956. That year at the Ideal Home Exhibition the house-builder Wimpey (different spelling!) displayed to a marvelling public its extremely well-equipped "house that every woman wants", selling at £2,195. But planners were intent on promoting "vertical living" in high-rise apartment blocks, in defiance of popular preference. The debate, almost a feud, between champions of high-rise and low-density rages even now, although the incurable British love of suburbia is winning – and the Green Belt, tragically, is losing!

Imbued with the same idealism and optimism that produced the National Health Service and the Festival of Britain in 1951, planners urged not merely the rebuilding but the entire replacement of what the blitz had destroyed, together with the rest of our antiquated city centres, too, as well as the whole of smug suburbia – that hated legacy of the inter-war years. Indeed, the modernist movement which was ignited by the War had already been smouldering for many years. As long ago as 1934, a young architectural correspondent had written:

"We must give up the rule which restricts the height of buildings, and we must not only do that, but we must build office blocks twice as high as St. Paul's, and have green spaces and wide roads in between.......Two dozen skyscrapers, though they would obviously dwarf St. Paul's, would not take away from its beauty if they were beautiful themselves. They would alter the skyline, certainly, yet we should not sacrifice health, time and comfort to one skyline because we have not the courage to create another."

This *avant-garde* barbarian was none other than John Betjeman, whom we all so fondly remember as the arch-conservationist and traditionalist, ferocious defender of ancient buildings and Poet Laureate of later life! Similarly, the Beveridge Report in 1943, which laid the foundations for the Welfare State, was celebrated by an exhibition at the National Gallery on "Rebuilding Britain', in the accompanying catalogue to which Sir William Beveridge wrote:

Ground-Breaking

"The very first thing to win is the Battle of Planning. We shall need to have planning on a national scale, boldly overstepping the traditional boundaries of urban council, rural council, County Council. Boldly overstepping the interests described so often as vested."

Whereas Winston Churchill commented, at one of his last Cabinet meetings, after listening to his ministers' commendations of the recent Town and Country Planning legislation:

"All this stuff about planning and compensation and betterment. Broad vistas and all that. But give me the 18th century alley, where foot-pads lurk, and the harlot plies her trade, and none of this new-fangled planning doctrine."

Well, there was no need to settle for one extreme or the other, but those opposite poles of opinion illustrate the vacuum that existed prior to creation of a market, which could not become institutionally established without a period of political stability, and certainly not until a capitalist economy was restored, operated by free private enterprise. Effectively, therefore, this market of ours was born with the return of a Conservative government in 1951 and evolved throughout that party's 13-years rule until 1964.

Ironically, however, the new prosperity of that period served to sustain the utopian delusions that persisted at municipal level. Witness the Liverpool City Centre Plan of 1965 by Graeme Shankland and Walter Bor, the plans in 1954 of their opposite numbers in Birmingham, Sheppard Fidler and Herbert Manzoni (whose 1952 plans for rebuilding the city envisaged three concentric ring roads intersected by thirteen radial roads), the visions of Patrick Abercrombie for the Clyde Valley and Edinburgh, and Colin Buchanan's prescriptions for traffic in towns everywhere, which would have destroyed the character and the spirit of these great, ancient places forever; but mercifully neither local nor central government could afford to pay for them. It was the final throes of this failed revolution that I unexpectedly encountered as late as the mid-60s in Edinburgh – see *Nicolson Street* and *Tollcross*. So planning and architectural opinion has come full circle within my lifetime.

Throughout these last 60 years, town planning authorities have always been unclear as to their priorities between three distinct roles: control (of what others want to do), conservation (of what others did long ago) and construction (of what the council itself wants to do). Some councils focus on *control* and *conservation* while others focus on *construction* – which can easily be confused with *campaigning*, having a socio-economic content and even a political bias. Their legacy – bureaucracy, endless revision of Local Plans,

Regional Plans and Development Plans, costs and delays of appeals and public inquiries, alienation of the electorate, demolition of most tower blocks of council flats built in the 1950s – 70s (many of which have not yet been paid for under Public Works Board 60-year loans) and sink council housing estates – is not one to boast about...... and now town and country planning is increasingly subjugated to politicised policies and controversies over power generation and transport.

All of this history I had to absorb quickly, while progressing at Way & Waller. In January 1955 I married the receptionist, whom I had first met on my flying visit for the interview. We had great fun keeping the romance secret – as we knew Mr Waller would disapprove – addressing each other formally during the day before meeting after hours for egg and chips costing 1s/9d (8.75p) at Flemings restaurant (nothing to do with the afore-mentioned hotel) which ran through from the NW corner of the Square to Oxford Street but was later turned into a huge Saxone /Lilley & Skinner shoe shop. We worked on Friday, married at Hampstead Register Office on Haverstock Hill on Saturday and I resumed as normal on Monday though my wife took the day off.

As feared, when Sam Waller learnt that we had married he was horrified. "But Linacre, she is the veritable nerve-centre of the whole firm, privy to partners' private business, whereas you are......" He did not actually say "the lowest form of life here" but that was what he meant. While not requesting that I resign, he plainly was not happy and, as my wife was earning £9 per week against my £8, her position had to be safeguarded. In any event, I wanted to progress to a real firm of surveyors where I could gain qualifications. The appointments pages of the *'Estates Gazette'* were full of opportunities, but I had no wish to become just another junior in a large West End or City firm, so applied to a small firm in Chase Side, Southgate, Hugh Davies & Partners, which seemed to offer ample scope. They wanted somebody to establish a 'Business Premises' department and were offering £500 p.a. plus use of a car plus commission on sales!

I got the job, and the Morris Minor; but there were two drawbacks, although neither bothered me. One was that we had bought a little house in Lime Grove, Shepherds Bush, so I had to drive all the way each day around the North Circular Road, but I quite enjoyed that and needed to improve my geography. The other was that I was expected to attend every Saturday morning to help the estate agents selling houses, though I enjoyed that too. But my main job was selling small retail businesses as going concerns, generally known as NewsConfTobs. In those distant days – pre-TV advertising, pre-supermarkets and retail parks, and pre-immigration – retailing throughout Britain was overwhelmingly in the hands of small independent shops. These were largely owned then by those who had fought in the War or were left unemployed after it, or by those who, having grown up during the War, wanted to make their own way in the world within striking distance of London. Often, of course, they had living accommodation above.

But financing these hectic transactions required as much skill and effort as negotiating the deal. If the properties were mortgageable – particularly with residential upper parts – but a gap of £500 or £1,000 still remained between what the buyer could raise and the price for the business (which consisted of the value of the freehold or lease, stock-in-trade and equipment, plus the nebulous element of "goodwill" – i.e. the notional capitalization of the suspected difference between official and actual profits which was laughingly called 'equity'), then I would take the applicant in a taxi to one of two or three wealthy money-lenders who would instantly arrange a 'second mortgage' at a dizzying rate of interest, the effect of which was often to turn the buyer into a seller within a matter of months.

I learnt a lot from Hugh Davies, a passionate golfer of Welsh extraction (close friend of Dai Rees, a Ryder Cup captain) and a big noise from Barnet to Cockfosters. After only a few months, however, Britain suffered a fuel crisis in the wake of the Suez debacle, when petrol rationing was imposed, condemning me to commuting by the underground and restricting business travel.

Much worse, HD summoned me one morning to advise that his application for a Fidelity Bond in my name, which was necessary because I would be handling money paid as deposits (either towards the purchase of a property or as a first quarter's rent in advance) had been refused by the insurers, the Railway Passengers Assurance Company, a division of the North British & Mercantile Insurance Co. Ltd., following their receipt of references requested from my two previous employers, as required. This was shattering, but HD was very decent, while obliged to confirm that his firm's insurance policies would be jeopardized if they knowingly employed somebody in a fiduciary capacity who had been refused a Fidelity Bond, but giving me time to investigate and take legal advice.

The next day I took the afternoon off to meet my wife and consult a lawyer for the first time in my life. We had no idea how to go about it but, deep in thought, found ourselves wandering down Gloucester Place, where we happened to stop outside no. 74, the offices of Wilde Sapte & Co. "Let's go in", she said, so we did.

We tried to explain the nature of our business, and found ourselves – total strangers and clearly of no substance – ushered into the office of the senior partner, Mr G D Peters, who treated us as if we were valued old clients. It became clear that the reason for my rejection was a malicious reference from Mr Green, the gentleman-farmer for whom I had worked before leaving abruptly – as I had been obliged to do when this opportunity of employment in London had materialized – while wholly unaware that I was still the prime suspect in his eyes (but not in those of the police or anybody else) for a burglary that by a grisly coincidence he had suffered just before I quit, when his house was broken into and the safe emptied in his study – the room which he had let me use for my College of Estate Management correspondence course. This is lapsing into straight autobiography, but I could not omit this episode because it exposes the absence then of any employee protection or right of redress, affecting any ambitious young man's career, for – whatever the grievance – one had to put up with it or move on.

Mr Peters wrote to Mr Green on 14th September 1956.

"Dear Sir,

Mr V T Linacre

We have been consulted by the above Gentleman who we understand recently had occasion to apply for a Fidelity Bond from a Guarantee Society. We understand that our Client gave to the Society your name and address as one of his former employers and that his application was refused by the Society. There are no circumstances in connection with our client's past history which could possibly have led the Society to come to such a decision other than any information which may have been supplied to the Society by you and our client therefore is forced to the conclusion that some statement made by yourself has caused the Society to refuse his application. Our client has placed before us full information as to the circumstances of his employment with you and explained that at or near the end of that period an unexplained robbery took place at your premises which the Police, in spite of repeated efforts during the past two years, have been unable to bring home to any person.

We hope that you realize the seriousness of making any statement with regard to the character of our client which you are unable to substantiate. As you are well aware there is no shred of evidence which would cause the slightest suspicion in the matter to fall on our client. In view of the circumstances we think that our client is entitled to have full particulars of any statements which you have made to the above-mentioned Society concerning him so that he may be in a position to rebut any charges which may have been made. If it is found that any statements have been made which adversely affect our client's character we must ask that these should be unconditionally withdrawn. The delay in obtaining the necessary Bond is seriously affecting our client's prospects of obtaining an engagement and in these circumstances we must ask you to treat this matter as urgent. We should be glad to hear from you accordingly as soon as possible.

Yours faithfully,
Wilde Sapte."

He also sent a copy of that letter to the Fidelity Guarantee Department at the Railway Passengers Assurance Company; but gently confirmed to me that "your position is not a strong one as you have no means of compelling Mr Green to give you any information as to what he told the Insurance Company." Mr Peters received this reply dated 25th September from the Insurance Company.

"We have to acknowledge receipt of your letter of the 24th instant with enclosure. You will of course understand that we are unable to enter into any discussion whatsoever as to the reasons which influence us in connection with applications for Fidelity Guarantee Insurance.

Yours faithfully, N N Britten (Manager)."

Enclosing a copy with his letter of 1st October, Mr Peters commented: "I am afraid that it is impossible to force them to disclose any information with regard to their reasons for turning down the application. As I explained to you, although the results are exceedingly unjust, they are within their rights in refusing to do business and withholding their reasons for doing so. I am writing again to Mr Green who has not so far answered my letter." There was nothing more he could do. Mr Green had evidently perpetrated a criminal libel against me but he was fully protected by the insurance company and consequently I faced losing my livelihood.

Mr Peters and I had become friends; he talked about his family – particularly his son in the City office at 18 Old Broad Street – and was almost as sorry as I to close the file, regretfully sending me a bill for just five pounds. Perhaps that quality of service inspired the growth of the firm, which soon amalgamated with another London practice to form Denton Wilde Sapte and after another fifty years merged with the US firm, Sonnenschein Nath & Rosenthal to become SNR Denton, one of the biggest law firms in the world, with 48 offices in 32 countries across 4 continents.

Meanwhile, as Mr Peters had suggested, I took the papers to a meeting with Frank Tomney, MP for our constituency of Hammersmith North, reputedly a thoroughly decent and hard-working back-bencher, in his office at 446 Uxbridge Road. He made copious notes, muttered about consulting a constitutional lawyer, and wrote to me on 17th October: "I have had an opportunity of discussing the difficulties regarding your Fidelity Bond, and am informed that the position is substantially as stated by your Solicitors. I can appreciate your difficulties and regret not being able to be of further assistance to you. I am returning your papers herewith." Hugh Davies had been kept fully informed and, while disappointed, he was so impressed by my diligence, as well as by my performance at work to take a chance and carry on without the Bond. But what if the firm's insurers got wind and threatened to invalidate their policies? "We'll worry about that if it happens", which was well-meant but no security. He even raised my basic salary to £12 per week, but it was time to move on. So back again to my weekly bible, the *'Estates Gazette'*, and there it was!

3 ARRIVAL

The pre-eminent firm of UK commercial property surveyors then was Healey & Baker. They were closely followed by Hillier Parker May & Rowden, Richard Ellis and Jones Lang Wootton, but H&B was top of the premier league. But this was only an emerging market to cater for a new sector, with no real impact yet on the economy, on property prices or institutional investment. It was simply the case that these 'Big Four' captured the bulk of the instructions by virtue of their spread of expertise and depth of records. H&B took the lead by concentrating on retail property from the start. Half of what I know today about property I learnt in four years and four months there, from November 56 to March 61.

I possibly made a colossal mistake quitting then, for if I had stayed I would surely have risen to a senior partnership within the next twenty years, made a great deal of money, and avoided the several errors of judgment that I made at later crises in my irregular career. But I would also have drunk too much, would not have devoted as much love and attention to my growing family, would not now have felt this consuming urge to write, and would probably have died long ago, as have almost all of my contemporaries.

In those days the whole of H&B was under one roof in St George Street, Hanover Square, barely a furlong from Way & Waller (which by this time had been taken over by a Newcastle firm, Storey Sons & Parker, who needed a London office, principally as a show-case for their new business pioneering the development and sale of villas abroad). The advertisement was for a junior negotiator in the London suburban shops department – right up my street! As it transpired, they actually had two vacancies: one for North Suburban and one for South. I applied and got an interview with the terrifying figure of Mervyn Orchard-Lisle. He had served as a high-ranking officer in the Royal Marines, and the setting was as unnerving as his physical presence, for it was dark by 5.30pm when I was ushered into his room, with only one lamp on a table and two chairs where we sat; but I was not intimidated and he let me prattle about my biggest deals in the wilds of Wood Green and Potters Bar, his obscured face concealing any suppressed laughter. He offered me the appointment for North Suburban immediately, without a second interview or even requiring references, at a starting salary of £750: £15 a week! But what mattered more than the money was that I had arrived at Mecca. I emerged into a very wet night, without a coat, but didn't notice the weather and had walked in a dream as far as Queensway before realizing that I ought to find a call-box to let my wife know of my jubilation and that I would be home in half an hour.

The firm, I soon discovered, was owned by four partners: in reverse order of seniority, Mervyn, who was the agency supremo, his elder brother Aubrey, responsible for all the specialist ("professional") departments and also for dealings with public buildings and government bodies, Douglas Tovey, a showman, great publicist and strategist, friend of property tycoons like Jack Cotton and Charles Clore, Harry Hyams and Joe Levy, as well as retailing tycoons like Hugh Fraser, Garfield Weston, Isaac Wolfson, Israel Sieff and Simon Marks; and the Chairman, Arthur Hemens, who conducted the auctions and cultivated the City.

Hemens liked to impress upon new boys the dangers of careless talk, telling how as a very young man he overheard in the bar of the club to which he had just been introduced by his father, one member boasting to another of the big deal that he had been offered, whereupon Hemens had walked out and proceeded to pull it off himself. In my first year I learnt unofficially that the fee turnover hit £1 million for the first time, of which total costs would have accounted for less than two-thirds, leaving over one third of a million among those four – immense wealth at the time.

Total staff numbered just 150, covering the entire British Isles and every branch of the profession, creating an intensely stimulating hothouse ambience. (Now they are part of the US-owned Cushman & Wakefield with a staff of over 14,000 in 60 countries). The advantages of such a compact outfit were that whoever dealt with Manchester could solve a problem by conferring with his counterpart covering Liverpool or Sheffield, whilst all the specialists – building surveyors, valuation, property management, legal, financial, rating, offices, industrial, residential, etc. – were readily to hand.

I say "his", by the way, because the entire fee-earning staff was male – the idea of a female surveyor was inconceivable – whereas the entire support staff below executive level was female. No unseemly behaviour was tolerated. But thanks to these strict standards, which were happily recognized and accepted, absolute trust and camaraderie prevailed in all quarters, without benefit of a 'Director of Human Resources'— a breed as yet unheard of. The backroom sorority was like an enclosed community, while all hundred or so of us men were totally committed both to mutual support and ferocious competition. Once, when downstairs in the filing rooms at 12.30 I saw one of the girls rushing about, wailing "Have you seen Doris? I haven't said goodbye to her" – yet she was only going out for lunch. As all communications and records were on paper, the filing system was vast and highly organized – as were the mail rooms. Sacks of morning post collected at 8.00, sorted and distributed around the building before 9.00, the formal working day starting with the ceremony of opening the mail at departmental conferences ('morning prayers') shortly thereafter, and instructions issued for immediate execution. Everything done by direct personal contact and without a minute's delay – no need for computers, emails, mobile phones or texting – and everybody knew what was happening instantly – news of big fee cheques (as well as of complaints) circulating throughout the firm by mid-morning. Transparency, knowledge, action were the watchwords – far more creative, effective and economical than the paraphernalia of today's IT.

Our outgoing correspondence was generated by Dictaphone, each filled plastic Dictabelt sent in a folder, with a note indicating the length and title of the items it contained, to the typing pool for transcription. The 'dragon' in charge of the stenographers wielded great power because she decided the order of priority for allocation of the work as the streams of folders were handed in to her overseeing cubicle. (The most indecent remark I have heard in my life – more shocking than the worst of the imprecations shouted by my RAF drill sergeant – was uttered with kind intent by a very nice young lady – which made it all the more shocking – who first took me round the building and on entering the typing pool said, "Sorry about the smell of fish – the girls have got their rags on." *I do wish I could forget that.*) The dragon kept a monthly tally of folders received from each of us, for presentation to the partners, which was intended as an index of productivity but placed a premium on verbosity and prolixity – on communication at the expense of performance.

Much of the output consisted of inter-office memos, intended for some response or action, plus copies circulated to those indirectly concerned, intended merely to be read and filed; but one rising star owed his progress largely to exploiting every opportunity, not only of composing responses to copy memos for the attention of the originators and others who had received copies, but also by adding names to the circulation list of anybody else who could be remotely interested or whom he wanted to learn his views, while inviting their comments to which he in turn responded.

Discipline and enterprise was another pair of complementary watchwords: hands tied inside the office but a free hand outside. Bowler hats were obligatory: arriving at the office, if the sergeant at the door noticed that anyone was neither wearing nor carrying a bowler he was instantly sent home and a deduction made from that month's salary. It had to be bought at Lock's in St James's, who presumably still have my wooden last in their dungeons, and the junior echelons could only wear the plain variety that soon became shiny and was put out into the garden as a nesting box, but promotion to higher rank conferred the privilege of acquiring the type with a soft pile. Also, only black leather shoes were permitted, except for brown shoes on Fridays to show (or pretend) that one was off to the country for the weekend, which accordingly we all did.

Two important functionaries, to whom we all paid court, were Mr Merry and Miss/Mrs ['Ms' not yet invented] Davy/Davie. He was responsible for cars, cameras and measuring tapes – which were 1 chain in length (i.e. 22 yards, 66ft, 4 rods, 100 links), beautifully made in leather cases with brass winders. In the Home Counties, as they were quaintly known, I hardly ever needed a car, but a camera and tape were two essential tools, of which he had discretion to supply models that were as new or due for replacement. Ms Davie/Davy was in charge of 'key plans', i.e. diagrammatic plans of every shopping street in the country, hand-drawn, simply indicating the occupiers with street numbers, the street frontages roughly to scale. Very long and/or important streets took more than one sheet. She kept the negatives from which prints were run off to order: a major operation as hundreds were supplied every day, either to enclose with correspondence (often mass-mailings) or to equip all who were setting off to visit any centre, in order to bring it up to date – it was an offence to arrive at or even pass through a location without checking the key-plan – so that every day she would have to deal with scores of us on returning that afternoon or the next morning, to note the changes in each case, all of which would then had to be transcribed onto the negative with the revision dates.

We almost all smoked throughout the day. But once, when summoned to the office of C. E. Williamson, the partner in charge of London shops, i.e. three levels above me, I tapped on his door, hearing him on the telephone but loudly bidding me enter and then waving me to sit down while he continued talking and smoking. So I also lit up – to give me something to do rather than appear to be listening to his agitated discussion – whereupon, having slammed down the 'phone and furiously waving the other hand in the air, still holding his cigarette, he railed: "Linacre, I particularly wanted to see you about something, but now there's something else which I'll deal with first. When entering a partner's room and invited to sit down, you do not light a cigarette without express permission – is that clear? Now, you've made me forget what I wanted to see you about......"

Cigarettes were indeed a form of currency. One prominent commercial property investor, Archie Sherman, who loved picking up deals from his favourite young agents, used to summon us London practitioners individually to his office on Hay Hill off Berkeley Square during the pre-Christmas season, to thank each of us for what we had done or tried to do for him during the year, and rewarding us according to his judgment of our performance by handing out a box of 500 cigarettes as his platinum award or 250 for gold or 100 for silver or 50 for bronze down to just "Best Wishes and let's hope for a more successful New Year" – or, of course, no invitation at all. We all indulged him in this ritual humiliation, treating the indignity of it as a joke; for he meant well and was, besides, a public philanthropist of note.

While every initiative was encouraged with minimal routine procedures – we were simply told what to do and left to get on with it – expenses had to be accounted for in detail. In that respect, office discipline reached out across the country. One poor chap, the East Midlands no.2, on returning from a three-day safari, had to hurry the paper-work including his expense-sheets, in which, trying to recollect his precise movements in Leicester, he automatically entered a nominal "Car-park 6d [2.5p]"— there were no street-parking meters in "the provinces" then, so most local authorities operated quasi-monopolistic civic car-parks. Unluckily a senior partner happened to have read that the Leicester City Council had recently appointed a new Planning Officer from Europe who wanted to try an experiment, which happened to be held that week, cancelling all car-park charges in order to observe and analyze the consequences. The poor chap was instantly dismissed, *pour encourager les autres.*

Equal ruthlessness was shown, shortly before Christmas of all times, to a regional no.1 who had occasional access to the office of his partner-in-charge, and could not resist taking a squint at the lists of proposed annual salary changes which were reliably rumoured to be circulating under confidential cover for partners' approval. On the desk and barely concealed, where they should not have been left, my friend was able very quickly to glance at the figures for his department and creep out. But his blunder, when they were in the 'Mason's Arms' round the corner and, as always at that time of year, speculating about salary increases, was to confide in a junior colleague that he "had heard" (as he put it) that the junior was getting only say £100 increase unlike 'X' on the same scale who would be getting £200, with the result that when in due course we were each called in for interview and told our fate, the young innocent, on being informed that he would be getting just £2 a week raise but urged to not to be disheartened (and warned as we all were not in any circumstances to divulge this information or discuss it with anybody), could not help blurting out: "But, Sir, why am I getting only £100 when 'X' is getting £200?" Whereupon the partner's face turned to stone, and of course it all came out – and my friend the departmental senior was fired on the spot.

The dawn of the 'swinging sixties' had not yet broken, but it was in the air. After a long post-war period of austerity, once rationing was finished and we had recovered from the shock of the Suez debacle, suddenly it was the revolutionary age of the E-type Jag and the Mini and the mini-skirt. Perfunctory strip-tease was performed in a few Mayfair pubs on the bar carpet around 6.00pm, arousing more embarrassment than lust or thirst, as the landlords tried to stretch the rush-hour by anything new that they felt the local magistrates would tolerate. Tommy Steele was playing in the "2 ii's" cafe in Compton Street and I was running around in taxis with Mary Quant and Vidal Sassoon (he was just my age), looking at possible premises in Chelsea and Kensington.

I must explain that Northern and Southern Suburbs were divided simply by the River, and that the North's territory started at Hyde Park Corner and Marble Arch, so that, incredibly, Brompton Road and Knightsbridge were 'suburban', as were Edgware Road, Marylebone High Street and Baker Street! The notional border ran round the North side of Holborn to skirt the City at the Angel, Islington, not that anybody ever ventured that far east. The reason for this extremely intrusive delineation of suburbia was simply a matter of priorities. Firstly, such an overwhelming volume of business grew out of Westminster that every block – almost every property – requiring special data and experience. Secondly, with such disproportionately high values, exclusive concentration on this core of central area was imperative. Thirdly, an imaginary intermediate zone between central and suburban could never be defined, because the inner and outer boundaries would be forever changing. Accordingly, one man was entirely devoted to Oxford Street while others specialized full-time on Bond Street, Piccadilly and Regent Street, Shaftesbury Avenue and Charing Cross Road, Covent Garden and The Strand, etc. My squad of six, conversely, spread out into the wilds of Middlesex, Hertfordshire and Essex, as far as business might take us.

Retail property predominated in both agency and investment, not only because it was booming, thanks to the insatiable public appetite for consumer and durable goods alike, but also because the other two sectors, offices and industrial, were twin Cinderellas – or, rather, the Ugly Sisters. (I am excluding residential altogether, because that sector was of no interest either for investment or development, thanks to the Rent Restriction Acts.) Market confidence in rental values and investment yields for offices outside the super-prime locations was highly volatile until the 1960s and for manufacturing and warehouse space until even later. It was the electronic revolution that stabilized the market in office-space and likewise computer-controlled storage and distribution plus the European-wide motorway network that brought the industrial property market to maturity. Besides, industrial property had always been regarded as the preserve of a few specialist firms in the City and a mystery to everybody else.

Offices, although an integral activity of commercial property surveyors, were very much an ancillary class of business, because the vast bulk of surviving purpose-built offices in central London (mainly in the City) were fifty or a hundred years old and more or less worn out; or else, as throughout the West End, occupied what were originally built as residential properties – all, therefore, severely deficient in scale, in technology, amenities, and hence of low rental value – particularly in relation to building costs which were still very high because of continuing shortages of materials. A cleared bomb site was worth more for use as a car-park than for redevelopment. The new Town Planning system, moreover, could not yet think three-dimensionally – 'skyscrapers' were still alien to London, where the height of a proposed new building was considered in relation to nearby church spires. Until the town planning regime grew up and architects – as well as institutional investors – started taking developers seriously, there was insufficient scope for premier firms of surveyors to specialize in the offices sector.

Meanwhile, there was virtually no 'High Street' retailing in the City of London itself. I had thought its arrival inevitable and overdue, but top multiples did not in fact materialize on any scale for another thirty or more years. During a rare discussion with Arthur Hemens himself, I had the temerity to ask why the firm did not open a branch office in the City, at which he snorted with disgust: "Linacre, are you quite mad? Healey & Baker open an office in the East End?" It was just like one of those H M Bateman cartoons. That attitude, essentially, explained why retailers took so long to get there. But maybe the Wapping Revolution, Canary Wharf, Big Bang and the Docklands Light Railway – all of which happened much later – had to happen first to create the necessary scale and changes in lifestyle.

Arthur Hemens would ask partners to send any spare personnel into his office for briefing immediately prior to one of the firm's auctions, held usually in the London Auction Mart, when he was to take the rostrum. The lots consisted mainly of small to medium-sized shop or mixed commercial properties ("the dross") but sometimes with one or two spectacular properties ("the nuggets"). Incidentally, never having studied the subject, I still cannot distinguish between those being disposed of by auction (a) as a last resort because they had failed to sell in the open market and (b) as a priority because they would fetch more than by selling in the open market. At our rehearsal he would run through the catalogue, outlining his tactics for each lot and instructing us at random – we were to scatter about the room unobtrusively – what price to bid and when. This practice, designed to stimulate genuine bids and to help get the bidding past the reserve price, was known as 'puffing' – it saved the auctioneer when stuck from having to "take bids off the wall" but was of doubtful legality and the subject of recurrent debate in the 'Estates Gazette'.

An annual cricket match was held at Winchmore Hill between H&B and arch-rivals HPM&R. Our star was young Bill Read, a very fast bowler, who worked alongside me. Modestly insisting that he was employed for no other purpose than to skittle out the enemy, he did that one year (probably in 1956, just before I joined) by taking all ten wickets, and was later presented with the ball mounted on a trophy. He also made recordings on Dictabelts – which soon whizzed round the building -- of his remarkable impersonations of several highly distinctive singers, celebrated then, such as Eartha Kitt, Mel Torme and Yma Sumac. By the way, HPM&R was known in the trade as *Hurry Panic Muddle & Rush*, just as Frank Knight & Rutley was known as *Knife Fork & Cutlery* and the very posh firm Debenham Tewson & Chinnocks (an ancestor of DTZ) as *Debutantes Toothsome & Chinless*.

Another welcome diversion was the annual 'Second XI Lunch' held at the Paviours Arms on the Embankment. This was for all fee-earners below the rank of Departmental Head. In 1958, it fell to me to organize, with the help of Sheila Goodwin and John Wills – who was clearly destined for the partnership. The theory was that I would produce some novel ideas for the entertainment while he would restrain me and she would take care of the girls. I had then been with the firm barely two years but was in a hurry. The objective of all at my level was to reach a salary of £1,000 a year by the age of 30, and I had just made it.

One huge difference within the profession was that graduate entry was the rare exception not the norm. Only a few had gained a B.Sc. in Estate Management, most of them by evening classes and correspondence courses, as I had begun in Scotland. Cambridge University's degrees in Land Economy mainly catered for those destined to manage country estates or play rugby for England. Now the old College of Estate Management is a vast institution at Reading University, while most provincial universities, especially former technical colleges, offer honours degree courses that are of widely varying quality.

The Estates Profession

So the majority had to devote spare time to study until ready to sit direct examinations for the Royal Institution of Chartered Surveyors, Chartered Auctioneers & Estate Agents Institute or Incorporated Society of Auctioneers & Landed Property Agents. There was additionally the Valuers Institution for those who had not gained qualifications, but gradually they too became respectable, introducing examinations, until eventually absorbed into ISALPA to form the Incorporated Society of Valuers & Auctioneers; while the CAEAI amalgamated with the RICS.

Thereupon a new body sprang up to cater for those remaining who were unqualified but with aspirations, the National Association of Estate Agents (mainly for agents in the housing market), which ironically, because its name was so much more easily remembered and because it was promotionally much more aggressive, became recognized and cultivated by the media and before long even by government as if it spoke for the entire profession, much to the fury of the established bodies' hierarchies. Ultimately, the ISVA was taken over by the RICS to create a quasi-monopoly, membership of which is the end-product of the requisite university training; while the NAES in turn introduced examinations to join the establishment without losing its independence.

But even today it is not a statutorily registered profession, i.e. not restricted to qualified practitioners, so a "closed shop" cannot be enforced, and consequently many who are fully qualified resent the restrictions imposed by their professional bodies which impede competition with the unqualified, who are free to pursue purely commercial practices, especially in the housing market. It is interesting that both the architectural and accountancy professions went through the same evolutionary process, and face the same problem – i.e. anybody can call himself an 'Architect' or an 'Accountant' or an 'Estate Agent', but ***not*** a 'Doctor' or a 'Dentist'. However, at H&B the issue was, literarily academic, for we were expected to have the necessary attitude and aptitude to learn on the job. Every hour working there was in itself intensive training.

Immediately on joining H&B I had flung myself into the activities of the ISALPA, within weeks was elected Hon. Sec. of the London Junior Centre (i.e. for the under-35 year-olds), and thereupon instantly busy organizing, with the Chairman, Richard Simpson of William Willett's, what, as it happened, was the first public meeting on the epoch-making and hugely controversial Rent Act of 1957, which – being naively ambitious – we held in the magnificent Church House, Westminster, and, as it turned out, very nearly on the date that the Act received the Royal Assent, while protesters demonstrated outside.

The speakers, moreover, were Britain's two most eminent authorities on this sphere of legislation, whom we had engaged with the insouciance of youth: R. E. (later Sir Richard) Megarry QC, author of *'A Handbook to the Rent Acts'* (1939) as well as of *'A Manual of the Law of Real Property'* (1946), etc., and Lionel Blundell QC, whose name was synonymous with the law of Landlord and Tenant (the 1954 Act was still highly topical). Actually it wasn't difficult, as they were both dying to speak on the burning issue of the Rent Act and we fortuitously bagged them first. It was a sell-out, and did me no harm at all with H&B.

The RICS and ISVA laid down a fixed scale of fees chargeable on valuations and commission chargeable on sales and purchases, which now looks so derisory yet was still in force as late as the 1970s. On valuation of a freehold property (i.e. excluding a structural survey), the amount of fee was 1% on the first £1,500, 0.5% on the next £11,000 and 0.25% on the residue; while for a leasehold property exactly the same *plus* 7.5% of the first £300 of annual rent payable under the lease, 4.5% on the next £700, 3% on the next £1,500 and 2% on the residue of the rent. On purchase of a property that had been sought and found and negotiated (which was my almost exclusive concern on behalf of multiple retailers), commission represented 2.5% on the first £5,000, 1.5% on the next £10,000 and 1% on the residue, with a minimum fee of £10. Sale commissions were slightly higher but of course involved greater liabilities and abortive work. So the commission on one of my big deals, the purchase of a freehold shop property (a whole building) on Earl's Court Road for Sketchley's the Cleaners at a price of £50,000 amounted to £625; but that was before the Great Inflation – several lifetimes ago!

The other successful applicant who started with me, having replied to the same advertisement and taken the vacancy for South Suburban, Robin Trueblood, also had the same birthday as me but born two years earlier. We became great friends. When he and his wife Una bought a semi-detached bungalow (i.e. having a bedroom upstairs with a dormer window in the roof) on a new little estate at Sandhurst in Berkshire, he suggested we might also like one, as he knew we were thinking of moving out of London, so we followed suit in September 1958.

This is a partial account of the property market's early years, not an autobiography, but it is relevant to explain that what my prospective wife and I had bought in January 1955, in Lime Grove, Shepherd's Bush. Although a whole terraced house, it was more precisely a 'part-possession leasehold'; i.e. the unexpired term of some 45 years of the original 99 years lease, subject to a ground-rent of something like £5 per annum and also to tenants, an elderly couple occupying the two rooms plus kitchenette and tiny bathroom comprising the whole ground except for the front hall, for which the rent – controlled by the Rent Restriction Acts – was about 25s/-d [£1.25] per week; and they also had exclusive enjoyment of the small back garden, to which my wife and I did not have access.

So we had vacant possession of only the upper parts, comprising two rooms, k & b, on the 1st floor plus a 2nd floor back addition providing a bed-sitting room, kitchenette & shower. For that I paid £1,600, securing a £1,200 mortgage from a local (Westbourne) building society at a relatively high rate of interest to reflect the leasehold tenure and protected tenants as well as my low earnings, borrowing the £400 deposit from my prospective mother-in-law. However, the rent from downstairs covered the rates on the property (to which the controlled tenants made no contribution), while mortgage repayments were covered by rent from tenants of the 2nd floor apartment which we let to overseas students whom I recruited from a very grateful British Council office in Hanover Street, round the corner from our place of work.

That worked well for over three years, but the family was growing fast, another was on the way, our accommodation was inadequate, the district was shabby (although Holland Park in one direction and Ravenscourt Park in another were both within pram-pushing distance) and the air unhealthy – we suffered thick fogs every winter – for all of which reasons, plus of course the sheer desire to get on, we pursued Trueblood's suggestion of moving out to the country. Our place sold easily enough, at a sufficient profit to repay mother-in-law. Lime Grove had a certain cachet because of the famous BBC studios fifty yards down on the same side – its buildings extending immediately behind our back garden and beyond through to Shepherds Bush Green.

But financially the decision to sell Lime Grove proved a colossal long-term blunder. If only I had been more aware of the housing market or if there had been somebody to give advice, we would have put up with the domestic inconvenience for another year or two, because (a) the controlled tenants could not both survive long and as soon as one passed on the other was bound to go into a home or family care, and (b) leasehold enfranchisement in the near future was inevitable, whereby owners of long leases would acquire the right to acquire the freehold at a price fixed by a multiplier of the ground rent, possibly factoring in the remaining length of lease. Both of these events came about, to the enormous benefit of our (successive) successors. Had we remained and become the owners of the unencumbered freehold, the property would have been worth even then over £10,000, giving us a net profit of some £8,000, say £250,000 in today's money; but that is ignoring real growth in value, for today the house would be worth double that. At the time, so early in family life, those gains from vacant possession and from emancipation of tenure would have transformed our fortunes. The only consolation is that none of this struck me until many years later.

So followed two-and-a-half years' commuting from Sandhurst via Camberley to Victoria Station, travelling in most mornings with Trueblood, I smoking one of his cigarettes on the train then he one of mine, either a 'Nelson' or an 'Olivier' – yes, the greatest actor of the age unwittingly promoting lung cancer. Robin's wife Una became godmother to our next son who arrived before our first Christmas there. She also travelled up to town each day but by different trains to the City, where she worked as private secretary to Ian Fleming, then Foreign News Editor of *'The Sunday Times'* but also busy writing the first James Bond novels, of which she typed the drafts that we were able to read privately, to our great excitement, as much on account of the tight security as of what we were reading. (A short while ago, having heard nothing of the Truebloods for over forty years, I suddenly saw her on 'The Antiques Roadshow', presenting for expert valuation a complete set of first editions, all with his autographed dedication to her.)

The main job of everybody at my level was to canvass the owners of privately owned shops occupying prime pitches in the centres covered by our respective territories, to persuade them to sell, in order to satisfy the insatiable demand from multiple retailers in that explosively expansionist era. That meant calling in person (not cold calling by telephone!), pounding the pavements day after day and visiting possible prospects month after month if necessary, cultivating the owners, understanding their business and personal circumstances while gathering and carefully recording details of the property as well as of their solicitors and accountants, converting them from potential to prospective vendors and then starting to negotiate terms. On average we each had about a couple of dozen main centres to cover, which meant that each one could be canvassed about twice a year. We kept registers of requirements for every High Street multiple retailer, indicating the gaps in representation they were anxious to fill and their relative priorities; but I never had to worry about identifying the client or even wondering who that might be, because it was invariably whichever retailer happened to be most important to the firm at that time or the one who would be most upset if it were learnt that we had secured such and such a unit in that particular centre and offered it elsewhere.

If I had to canvass by letter because the owners of a target property were not personally accessible, I was obliged to incorporate a "saver clause", asking them to pass my letter to any solicitor, accountant or surveyor who might act for them. This was to protect us against a charge of 'touting' or 'soliciting', which was an offence so grave as to risk expulsion from the professional bodies. That, once again, reflected the pretence that we were purely professional rather than commercial practitioners. Not once in my experience did any owners of a target property pass such a letter to their professional advisers, except where coincidentally they were intending to sell and had already instructed agents. Generally, they either got in touch personally, if only out of curiosity (which opened the door), or ignored the letter altogether, but maybe kept it on file. Nevertheless, most august firms of surveyors occasionally found themselves appearing before Disciplinary Committees if one of their negotiators forgot the precious 'saver clause' in a letter received by a hostile or mischievous proprietor or that fell into the hands of a proprietor's solicitors or rival surveyors. So canvassing in person was far more enlightening and productive. I could spend a long day in Watford or Golders Green, slogging up and down the main street, conducting a dozen interviews but returning empty-handed; yet that was still well worth-while because I would have moved half of them forward and next time, five or six months later, one or two should start talking – or one of them might even get in touch meanwhile. When I did come back rejoicing, with the news that

Smiths at no. xx was willing to sell for £xxx, subject to special conditions (a) (b) (y) & (z), the partner would immediately call a departmental meeting to decide: "Right, who is due a big favour?"

Every major suburb then boasted a department store, often family-owned, but I was not yet competent to deal with any. I do remember, however, collaborating with Robin Trueblood on an analysis of rental values (actual or notional) for department stores around London, and arriving at an astonishingly consistent rule-of-thumb of 15s/- [75p] per square foot overall. No doubt a gross over-simplification, but of more than academic interest as an indicator of viability, relating rental value to turnover rather than merely to floor area.

A far-sighted managing Director of Selfridges declared in the *Financial Times* in 1955 that it was only through "providing an environment and attractions, which convert shopping from a chore to an interesting relaxation" that they could hope to win back trade. The first department store to use television for advertising its January sale was Beatties of Wolverhampton in 1957.

In central London, although several department stores still flourished, and a few names have survived vestigially, most have since disappeared: Barkers, Derry & Toms, Pontings, Marshall & Snelgrove, Bourne & Hollingsworth, Gorringes, Peter Robinson, Army & Navy, Whiteleys, Penberthys & Jays, while Debenham & Freebodys was reincarnated. When in 1956 the very traditional Whiteleys in Bayswater daringly introduced self-service departments its bourgeois clientele revolted, forcing the restoration of counters; a reversal from which the business never recovered.

At the height of the mania generated by Hugh Fraser's and Charles Clore's spectacular acquisitions, with which Douglas Tovey was closely associated, I circulated a ditty, modelled on a Bing Crosby-Bob Hope duet, which provoked a mixed response, this being the verse in question:

Oh Mr Fraser, / Yes, Mr Clore, / I hear that you've been buying stores galore? / Yes, but I'm in something of a mess / As I've just bought M & S. / Marks & Spencer's, Mr Fraser?/ Marshall & Snelgrove, Mr Clore!

Clore was assembling the British Shoe Corporation; acquiring True-form, Freeman Hardy & Willis, Dolcis, Manfield, Phillips, Curtess, and eventually Saxone and Lilley & Skinner, with most of which H&B was much involved. British shoe manufacturing (mainly based in Northampton apart from Clarks in Somerset) was killed in the 80s by abandonment of leather in favour of casual footwear, especially 'trainers' and other cheap imports, but until then it boomed, channelled through the expansion of these retail chains, greatly facilitated by Clore's perfection of the 'lease-back' technique. In precisely the same way that to Max Joseph the business of hotels basically consisted of "letting space at a premium", to Charles Clore the business of shoe retailing was generating revenue to pay rent in order to release the capital value of the property.

So he would buy a multiple brand and sell the freeholds to a pension fund or insurance company in return for occupational leases, typically for 21 years, at full 'rack rents', showing the investors a good return, while revealing within a few years of trading performance which branches could afford market rents and which could not – the former perhaps earning refurbishment or enlargement and the latter being sold. I recall his predicting that Woolworths, which ever since the 1930s had been and still was 'King of the High Street', would collapse if it ever ceased to concentrate solely on merchandising – which is what it excelled at – and allowed its attention to be distracted by the realization that, with a vast collection of freeholds, all in prime locations, it had inadvertently become one of the biggest property companies in the country; i.e. that any current open market revaluation would demonstrate that many of its branches, while apparently flourishing and for accounting purposes highly profitable, would be unable to pay a full 'rack rent' under a modern lease to show an adequate return on the value of the freehold. Fifty years later Clore was proved right.

This 'lease-back' technique was often confused with 'asset-stripping' and condemned as such, but it was not a case of making a killing by breaking up the business to dispose of its parts, but rather of releasing the capital value of the properties in order to put the retailing business on an efficient, competitive footing. However, the freehold sales often did more than recoup the cost of acquiring the company, while the brand name became purely ornamental as the company effectively disappeared.

Parts of the epoch-making Landlord and Tenant Act of 1954, which had come into force while I was at Way & Waller, reflected this new recognition of real estate values as a major factor in the life and conduct of commerce, industry, financial services and government – and the need to justify those values by making the real estate "earn its keep". Land, of course, had throughout history been regarded as a hoard and prime measure of wealth and rank, but in this new era it must have a value that varies according both to the national economic climate and, more particularly, to the income it produces.

For in this revolutionary period, shopping habits were about to be transformed by two pioneering developments. One was the phenomenon created by Jack Cohen, who had started selling from an East End market stall in 1919, bought a shipment of tea in 1924 from a Mr T. E. Stockwell, from whose initials, joined to the first letters of his own name, derived the brand of what became Britain's biggest and the world's third biggest retailer, Tesco, which in the late 1950s was still famous for its primitive slogan "pile 'em high and sell 'em cheap". With the rapid spread of television in the mid-late 50s, disused cinemas were becoming available for which there was no apparent alternative use, but providing large, well located buildings in good condition with solid open floors which, when gutted, were ideal for stacking boxes of cans, jars, cartons and bottles, bought in huge quantities, letting customers wander about and help themselves – a concept which was at first incomprehensible to millions, accustomed to queuing and to being served in specialist shops, but was soon grasped universally. The founder of supermarkets in Britain (though not in the USA where vast distances had long since demanded shopping in bulk by station wagons and shooting brakes from out of town markets and rural depots), Sir Jack was still very active in my day.

He had opened the first proper supermarket (as distinct from small, self-service stores) in Malden, Essex, in 1956; yet in 1957 British housewives were still making an average of 7.6 visits to the grocer and 3.3 visits to the butcher each week, partly because few owned refrigerators. Jack Cohen had bought several hundred established grocery stores by acquiring the Williams and Harrow chains, to which he added the Charles Phillips and Victor Value chains in the early 60s, converting all the larger premises to self-service and disposing of the units that were too small for that treatment. What vision! But it took another generation before my profession understood how to estimate and calculate their rental value or rate their investment yield.

Pedestrian Precincts

The other innovation was the equally fantastic notion of a covered pedestrian shopping street, which became known as a 'precinct'. The first in Britain was at Crossgates, near Leeds, which we all had to visit for the purpose of assessing its merits and prospects. The initial response generally was amusement: it would never work. Why should anyone want to desert the bustle and hubbub, the unique character of a High Street, for such a lifeless, anonymous, clinical place? Sir Simon Marks of Marks & Spencer was dismissive: in a verdict worthy of Sam Goldwyn, he declared, "You'll never get us into one of those precepts"! To the French and Italians, with their traditions of classical arcades and mediaeval pedestrian streets, they did not appear so alien, and in North America, again, the 'mall' was a natural development, forming a link between huge stores (the 'dumbbell principle) with masses of car-parking on cheap land. But in Britain, retailers and planners could never make up their minds – and really still haven't – *firstly* whether the intention is (a) to provide a complete range of specialist trades appropriate to the class and character of the centre, while ensuring their protection by avoiding duplication, *or* (b) to provide the public opportunities for comparison shopping by promoting an unrestricted letting policy – even, perhaps, creating a distinctive theme by concentrating several competing multiples in the same trade; and *secondly* whether (a) to emphasize the convenience of 'one-stop' shopping – park your car, do your shopping all under one roof and get away – or (b) to prolong visits by concentrating on catering and leisure facilities.

Both of these retailing earthquakes, the supermarket and the shopping precinct, erupted during my early tumultuous years at H&B. It was also in 1958 that word went incredulously round the office that two young surveyors had dared to quit the eminent Mayfair firms of commercial property agents where they had respectively qualified (Dudley Samuel & Harrison and Edward Erdman, as I recall) in order to set up on their own. What a nerve! Obviously they couldn't last. One was Neville Conrad and the other John Ritblat – aged 23! But within months, partners at H&B were telephoning the young men's secretaries to arrange meetings. Conrad, as I recall, became a developer with Regional Properties, while Ritblat not only took the firm of Conrad Ritblat into the premier league of commercial property agents but also created The British Land Company which grew into one of the biggest property development and investment companies in Europe; himself becoming President of the Company and, as Sir John, a foremost philanthropist and patron of the arts.

I had no experience of new shopping development up to that point. Two projects, both involving H&B, were getting under way within my territory, but they were a mystery to me. One was at Swiss Cottage, along Finchley Road beside the John Barnes department store. Which reminds me that further up Finchley Road was a superb continental delicatessen which was always busy and immensely popular in cosmopolitan Hampstead, especially its famous gateaux and other products of its boulangerie, as well as the confiserie, charcuterie, etc., behind a charming but dilapidated old shop-front which one day, unaccountably, the owners decided they had to replace with the latest style; so a week later it was unveiled, a gleaming aluminium and vitrolite horror; but the shock soon turned to laughter because, in a continuous band on a frieze above the main window were meticulously etched those exotic terms: 'delicatessen' 'charcuterie' 'confiserie' 'boulangerie' and finally 'gateauxs' *[sic]*! Word spread throughout NW3 and beyond: the mistake proved a PR master-stroke because from then on the place was known far and wide as 'Gateaux's' – pronounced as three syllables to rhyme with folks's – e.g. "I'll pop into Gateaux's on my way home." Foolishly it was scrapped a generation later.

The other impending project was something similar at Notting Hill Gate. Both of these schemes were conventionally built along the existing frontages of main roads. Neither showed a trace of imagination or advance in retail planning or design or regard for traffic or the environment. Even then I could readily see how much better they could have been by exploiting back-land and air-space.

However, I might have continued toiling in the inexhaustible quarry of Northern Suburbia indefinitely, until, in August 1958 (just after my 30th birthday), suddenly summoned to a meeting with Mervyn O-L. What had I done? But his proposition was fascinating. A colleague, Roderick Macfarlane Maclean, who covered Scotland – and who I therefore scarcely knew – was about to leave in order to return to his home town Edinburgh: would I like to succeed him? This was phenomenal promotion, for I had been with the firm less than two years. I realized that one reason for my selection was an Edinburgh school and university background: as M O-L jocularly put it, "you speak the language, don't you". He also aired his familiarity with Scots real estate law by commenting: "You know that sticking 'Subject to Contract' on a letter won't protect you there?" To which I nodded enthusiastically, despite knowing nothing of the sort.

The explanation for that legal quirk, by the way, is that every letter I sent from Way & Waller, Hugh Davies and H&B, relating to any property in England, was required to have that expression typed in bold caps at the foot or even in the subject heading, to emphasize that its contents were not to be construed as forming part of any contract; but in Scotland, as I was about to learn, any correspondence could be held to be binding unless the contrary was expressly stated in the body of the text – i.e. an apparently informal letter of offer and equally informal letter of acceptance could be treated as an "exchange of missives", constituting a binding contract – a useful first lesson.

So the following Monday I had to report to David Stephens, dubbed the 'Colonial Partner' because he was responsible for Scotland, Ireland and Wales. Less than five years after arriving in London, never imagining I would set foot North of the Border again except as a tourist, I was back working in Scotland.

4 ADVANCEMENT

The firm suffered a regular turnover of Scottish representatives, none lasting more than two or three years, because of two unique disabilities. One, obviously, was geographical, the distance from London and size of the territory. The other was even harder to cope with: Scotland was effectively a foreign country with a different legal system affecting our whole sphere of operations – contract, land and property tenure, rating, planning and building regulations, professional practice – which isolated the lone Scottish standard-bearer from the armies in the South.

As Maclean had a transitional fortnight, Stephens told him to take me on a week's lightning familiarisation tour of the main centres in the country, omitting only two areas: the South West – Ayr, Kilmarnock & Dumfries – because we hadn't time, and several of the old industrial satellites of Glasgow, because they seemed uniformly depressing. Maclean tried to point out significant properties under current negotiations everywhere, but it was too much and too strange for me to absorb; and anyhow, understandably, he was equally concerned to exploit the opportunity of calling on as many of his contacts as possible to acquaint them with his forthcoming move to Bernard Thorpe & Partners – it was a highly profitable trip for him, whatever I may have gained from it.

Once initiated and acclimatized, I had to memorize property values and details of ownerships in all the main streets of Scotland and, apart from dealing with work in progress passed on by Maclean and special new assignments handed down via David Stephens, make week-long trips that allowed time for detailed exploration of one city or group of towns in one region, revising the key-plans and calling on the obvious targets – familiar properties in prime locations that we knew from departmental records had been privately owned, in many cases for generations, and had withstood persistent overtures from my predecessors for many years. "Oh, another one – so what might your name be, then?" was the usual greeting.

Research was very much easier in Scotland than down South, for four reasons. First, each City, County and Burgh (equivalent of the English 'Borough') was its own rating authority, controlled by an official known as the Assessor who worked closely with the Treasurer or Chamberlain (today's Director of Finance), whereas in England the Inland Revenue had taken over the entire business of rating valuation for the whole country; so details of properties with names of proprietors and rateable values were printed in bound volumes known as the Assessor's Roll, open to public inspection. This accessibility and transparency of essential data was a huge advantage. Rateable values were called "assessed rentals", because the basis of valuation was a fair rent payable under a tenancy that was notionally renewable from year to year. Thus, having prepared the budget for next year, those two Officers would compare the amount of revenue required with the sum of the assessed rentals and declare the necessary "poundage", which would be e.g. 25 shillings (£1.25) if the revenue required was one-and-a-quarter times the sum of assessed rentals.

But the severe drawbacks were that (a) there was no incentive ever to conduct revaluations for the purpose of bringing assessed rentals up to date, because the declared poundage could simply increase with inflation of property values, so that eventually poundages were being declared of £3 or £4 in the pound, which made a nonsense of the system; and (b) it benefited wealthy authorities and penalized the poor, because those with high values required relatively low poundages and vice versa – this inequity being compounded by the far greater expenditure required on public services in poorer areas – giving rise to grotesque contrasts such as that between the tiny annual charge levied on a shop within the rich ancient counties of Selkirk, Roxburgh & Peebles and the crippling charge on one in Coatbridge or Clydebank. So the antiquated system which had never changed since the counties were mapped out according to the boundaries of Sheriffdoms, long before the Industrial Revolution, was eventually scrapped and centralized by the Inland Revenue as in England. But meanwhile it was a major consideration affecting rental and capital valuations in my business, although it just meant doing my homework from the information which was freely available.

The second reason why research was so much easier in Scotland was that the feudal system of tenure still prevailed, unreformed; meaning that over the whole country roughly two thirds of the shops in Main Streets were 'owner-occupied', i.e. were held on 'heritable' title (that could be inherited) directly from the 'feudal superior' who was in effect the ground landlord. There was no freehold ('fee simple absolute in possession' as in England): instead, all land was in theory held ultimately from the Sovereign – hence the universal term 'real estate', real meaning royal – who granted estates to the chief aristocrats, as reshuffled after the Jacobites' defeat in 1746. They or their estates became the feudal superiors, who in turn granted heritable title to 'tenants', as they were still known, even though they had perpetual title.

The original intention, which theoretically remained forever enforceable, was that tenants (heritable proprietors) were under obligation to improve and work the land if agricultural or to develop it if urban, generally by building on it and subsequently to pass it on to the next generation. In town and city centres, the estate owners (by now often institutions or charitable trusts) carried out large-scale development themselves, especially residential, as in the New Town of Edinburgh, then 'sub-infeudated' by selling the houses or flats, so that one 'tenement' could comprise a hundred dwellings, each privately owned.

But whether en bloc or individually, the title was subject to 'ground burdens' as set out in the 'feu charter', comprising (a) the equivalent of an English 'chief rent' or 'fee farm rent' – a perpetual fixed ground rent – called 'feu duty' which originally (maybe centuries earlier) represented a fair rental value of the land but over the centuries of course plummeted to relatively insignificant levels, yet still an item to be taken into consideration for valuation purposes; and (b) any restrictions on the permitted uses of the land or buildings which were generally archaic and irrelevant, and frequently at odds with present-day planning/ building/ public health regulations. Some of these title restrictions could be exploited by commercially ruthless estate managers ('factors'), who demand a premium ('grassum') as payment for a 'minute of waiver' to remove the restriction. This was money for nothing, as well as perverse and anti-social, since the restriction had been of no conceivable benefit to the estate for generations and therefore the estate could suffer no loss by its removal; and furthermore the existence of the restriction had often been completely forgotten until the proposed transaction in question had arisen, prompting resurrection of the estate deeds.

Typically, when I was instructed to sell a surplus branch of a bank with car-parking, which had been converted around 1920 (i.e. before 1947 when the need for planning permission for change of use was introduced) from what was originally a villa – i.e. a large house with a garden – in the centre of a town which had been a village before the surrounding coalfield was discovered, it was revealed that according to the title deeds the property was permitted to be used solely as "a dwelling-house with ground for grazing no more than one cow"; but nobody had realized it until then. That provided the feudal superior's zealous factor with an opportunity to 'milk the title-deeds' by exacting an arbitrary lump sum payment in return for a retrospective waiver. Such exploitation did not cease until abolition of the feudal system by a series of statutes concluding in 2000.

So my clients, almost invariably a multiple retailer based in England, needed a Scottish law firm to act as agents for its principal solicitors or legal department, to examine title deeds carefully before exchanging contracts ('concluding missives'). Where the client was venturing across the Border for the first time, I often had to recommend and brief a Scottish firm, who might well be experienced in dealing with big firms of London solicitors in connection with litigation or acting for public bodies or with institutions or stock-brokers, but might never have had to collaborate with solicitors in the retail sector. Furthermore, these national retailers' solicitors were usually based in English cities far from London, because most multiples were head-quartered in the provinces where they had originated and still retained their legal advisers there. In such cases the introduction sometimes proved a mutual culture shock.

Likewise, in the drafting of conditions attached to the offer to purchase, differences in fundamental principles – even in ethos or temperament – between English and Scots law quickly became apparent; because sixty years ago the Anglo-Saxon concept of 'reasonableness', of 'equity', was virtually meaningless or even unknown in Scotland. I am tempted to suggest, for the sake of making the point, that the Scots are a rigorously literal-minded race, and accordingly in Scots law a document means precisely what it says, no more and no less, permitting no variations in interpretation; whereas the English are a tolerant, pragmatic lot, allowing latitude and discretion by implication wherever practicable. Hence the Scottish exploitation of waivers; hence likewise the need to draft conditions very tightly to cover all possible contingencies. But I enjoyed this academic discipline – my university training at last proving useful – while the fact that by far the majority of town centre shops were owner-occupied remained a huge advantage in attacking this *terra nova* or *incognita*.

So also was the fact that almost all the others were held on annual tenancies, renewable from year to year – the theoretical basis for 'assessed rentals'. It was astonishing to discover that several large, old-established retail businesses, well fitted out and equipped, with a substantial goodwill value and inventory, flourished for generations on the strength of an annual tenancy with not the slightest qualm of insecurity. This was because (a) their landlord was often a trust or local property investor, whose sole interest was a safe inflation-proofed income, and (b) this had always been standard practice, since there was no alternative or middle way between annual tenancy and owner-occupation. The reason for that, of course, was that leasehold was still an alien Anglo-Saxon concept. The Landlord and Tenant Act of 1954, mentioned earlier, did not apply to Scotland, where property was either *in rem* or *in personam* – i.e. either real or personal – so that a leasehold, not being heritable, was merely personal, like any other chattel.

But with the invasion by multiple retailers and the first influx of property developers from London, this had to change; with the consequence that I spent the next few years assisting in the grafting of leasehold onto an inherently incompatible feudal system of tenure, a process with which many leaders of the Scottish legal profession were privately most unhappy, although most reluctantly admitted was inevitable. Certainly, the first generation of commercial town centre redevelopment and the creation of the first Scottish New Towns, all of whose financing depended on long head-leases and occupational under-leases, could never have happened under the old regime.

The third reason why preparatory homework was so much easier in Scotland was that H&B enjoyed an almost clear field. The only competition in the entire country consisted of Hillier Parker's small office in Edinburgh, run by Harold Barker, later assisted and succeeded by Colin Beckett (both having come up from the South) and a firm of residential property sales and management agents, Gumley & Davidson, also Edinburgh, with a commercial property department run by Logan Melville. Both firms were always welcoming and delighted to cooperate. It sounds incredible, but in the whole of Glasgow and the West of Scotland there was not one firm of surveyors specialising in commercial property. Well, it was only thirteen years since the end of the War, so professional practice generally had not noticeably changed since the 1930s. But the specific reason was the resistance – indeed hostility – by the entrenched legal profession to encroachment and usurpation by what it regarded as the piratical, even parasitical, parvenu and, worst of all, *'English'* trade of estate agency.

For the tradition in Scotland was to regard the lawyer as one's "man of affairs", who would take care not merely of one's legal affairs but also one's property and financial business. The City of Glasgow Corporation employed 72 qualified solicitors in its Town Clerk's Department before it eventually, to their consternation and bewilderment, decided around that same *annus mirabilis* of 1958 that it really needed to appoint an Estate Surveyor to advise on its commercial real estate assets and on new developments. He was a Glaswegian, congenial and popular, but resigned after a couple of years because the Town Clerk's army of lawyers refused to relinquish the necessary areas of authority and responsibility to permit an Estate Surveyor to function; creating an embarrassing uproar which compelled the executive officers to produce a proper remit with appropriate rank and status for the benefit of his successor.

The lawyers in the Town Clerk's Department of Edinburgh resisted even longer and gave the City's first Estate Surveyor a much harder time, for he was recruited from England and soon isolated, both socially and operationally, and after no more than three years apparently committed suicide, alone one night at his desk in his office up a mediaeval tenement stair in the High Street. (That was after my H&B period but relevant to add in the present context.) Even today, fierce rivalry exists between solicitors and estate agents in the house-sales agency; most Scottish law firms doubling as estate agents – for many, indeed, commissions from sales are vital to the firm's profitability.

So estate agency was regarded as the illegitimate offspring of the legal profession, just as town planning was regarded as the illegitimate offspring of architecture and, centuries earlier, architecture itself was regarded as the illegitimate offspring of the mason's craft. It is a natural process, which proliferates today with the emergence of so many new sub-specializations. But in Scotland the estates profession in Scotland, long after maturity, has barely recovered from its birth pangs. So it is ironic that law firms, while inclined to adopt a snobbish attitude towards estate agents, are nevertheless happy to describe *themselves* as "Solicitors and Estate Agents" to catch the business; whereas equally snobbish commercial property professionals hate the designation 'estate agents', insisting on the appellation 'surveyors', which many are not!

This whimsical digression was by way of elaborating on the reason why H&B faced so little competition in Scotland fifty-odd years ago. But only a fraction of the huge void caused by the dearth of commercial property specialists could be filled by the legal profession, as there were so many functions beyond the capabilities of even the most versatile and old-established firms of solicitors. In particular, full-time expertise was required in the valuation and management (including repairs, lettings and rent-collection) of the vast areas of four-storey tenement blocks which for a hundred years had housed the bulk of the working classes living around the heavy industries on which their livelihoods depended; principally in Glasgow and its satellites throughout the West of Scotland, Dundee and Edinburgh.

Where England had 'back-to-backs' – row upon row of two-storey terraced houses with the front door onto the street and a privy in the small back yard which opened onto a passage-way shared with the row facing the parallel street, Scotland had these teeming tenements which typically comprised sixteen dwellings entered from a common doorway and stair, four per floor, each consisting of only one or two rooms, with one privy on each landing. The population densities and standards of public health were horrific.

So a distinct profession of 'Factors and Valuators' had become established, peculiar to Scotland and very largely concentrated in these major centres, who were highly respectable and proficient, lending welcome diversification to the real estate profession; but they had no expertise in commercial property or in new development. Of course, not all tenements were slums – vast estates of sandstone tenements in Glasgow, granite in Aberdeen and ashlar in Edinburgh, are roomy, modernized, immaculate and, close to the city centre, increasingly popular and expensive – but it is the slums that are most vividly remembered, for they were at their very worst in the late 1950s when I started in Scotland, just before the huge clearance schemes got under way, along with the explosion of high-rise Council housing and creation of New Towns in the countryside. When staying overnight at an hotel in the Glasgow city centre on one of my first trips, the shock on going for an evening stroll across the river to explore the Gorbals district will stay with me forever.

This Victorian tradition of tenement housing in Scotland grew from a plentiful supply of stone in different varieties from local quarries which were ideal for multi-storey building (with no tradition of brick-making owing to a lack of clay) and the need to conserve heat in a more rigorous climate, but above all from the heritable system of tenure which facilitated multi-ownership – the creation of separate titles for numerous individual dwellings within one block – which is clearly impossible in England where each unit would have to be leased from a common freeholder or head lessee. With over-crowding, decay and neglect, the poorer tenements (the majority) were all rented, generally at no more than ten bob (50p) a week, while the better sort were owned, subject to a modest feu-duty and a fixed fraction, according to the number in the block, of liabilities for common repairs to the fabric (from the roof to the drains) and cleaning of the entrance and stair, etc.

But where the 'houses' (apartments) have all been sold off, it is often difficult or even impossible, in the absence of a single proprietor, to enforce these repairing, decorating, insuring and maintenance obligations against a multiplicity of owners; those living on the ground floor disputing the need for a proposed roof repair, those living on the top floor disputing the need for overhauling the drains, while any one owner might decline to pay in the hope that eventually all the others will give up and spread his share among themselves. This inherent defect in what is still an essentially feudal system of tenure is an unintended consequence of its emasculation by a series of modern 'reforms' which, principally by liquidating feu-duties, have destroyed the robust estate management role of 'superior landlords'.

Even worse, concerning the poorer tenements in the rented sector, there was little attempt at management beyond basic sanitation and keeping the entrance and stair swept, because the income did not justify it; so they spiralled into dilapidation, dereliction and demolition. It has become apparent, but only in retrospect, that mitigation of these deficiencies in the system of tenure was effectively a prime function of 'factors and valuators', but rendered more difficult to perform without collection of feu-duties; hence increasing reliance on statutory control and local authority enforcement for execution of common repairs.

Not only did H&B face little competition, but also – and this is the fourth and final reason why research was so much easier in Scotland – there were very few national multiple retailers established there. This was largely because of the heavy costs of delivery owing to the distances between the main centres in that pre-motorway age, and the consequent strength of exclusively regional chains which deterred attempted intrusion by nationals; but the main reason, once again, was the absence of available premises on a leasehold basis. Acquisitions on annual tenancies could not be considered, while acquisition of single heritable properties meant having to arrange a sale-and-lease-back or straight borrowing – as well as a careful search of ancient titles – all of which had long dissuaded Southern-based multiples from expanding across the Border.

Principal clients which were committed to such an expansion campaign had to adopt one of three strategies. They could produce a programme of acquisitions comprising a list of top priority centres on which to concentrate, with an estimated budget on the strength of which to arrange a line of financing; or, if the nature of the trade was appropriate, seek to take over a company that operated a regional chain which could then be reconditioned and rationalized, to provide a basis from which to expand across the country; or, in the case of large stores, to acquire adequate premises for one outlet as a pilot in a medium-sized town that did not contain an established business posing direct competition, in order to test consumer reaction – ideally in

Kirkcaldy which, as all socio-economic surveys at that time showed, was Scotland's 'average town' – i.e. if a newcomer or product did well there it could be safely rolled out across the country. (The corresponding 'average town' in England then was Reading.) Thus, Littlewoods was just opening its first branch in Scotland in premises on the High Street, acquired through my predecessor, Maclean. Kirkcaldy was known as the 'lang toon' because of its long main thoroughfare running parallel to the sea-front, facilitating my assembly of a site there for building the first British Home Stores ('BhS') branch in the country.

The last retail grocery empire prior to the supermarket revolution was Allied Suppliers, in England embracing such chains as Lipton, Maypole, Meadow Dairies, Perks Dairies, and Home & Colonial; in Scotland controlling four main regional groups – Massey, Templeton, Galbraith and Cochrane – all run independently, which suited the management, of course, but proved hopelessly inefficient in face of the threatening competition from supermarkets. The charming Scottish M.D., Charles Sykes (English, naturally), found it increasingly difficult to reconcile brand-loyalty with the huge potential benefits of centralized buying and distribution, as well as attempting to reconcile traditional high street and indeed corner shop trading with the onset of big stores and the demands of car-parking. After the shock of his first visit to the shopping centre in the New Town of Cumbernauld, a multi-storey concrete monstrosity built on a whale-back ridge, exposed to all the elements, he vowed never to repeat it as he could not find his way to their own brand-new store in this three-dimensional maze, but was obliged to retrace his steps back to the car-park, which was difficult enough, in order to set off again accompanied by his driver to escort him to the store.

The first supermarket in Scotland, by the way, was launched, surprisingly, by the Co-op, operated by its enterprising Edinburgh Society, St. Cuthbert's, located opposite the King's Theatre just up from Tollcross – with no car-parking. I well recall the public's initial reaction, which was no doubt universal: 'You mean that anybody can wander about and help themselves to whatever they want?'

One of H&B's biggest assignments periodically was to revalue every retail outlet in the group, numbering well over 3,000, of which a disproportionately large number were in Scotland (about 600 as I recall) on account of those regional chains. We were reissued with the completed inspection report from the previous exercise five or six years earlier, which saved most of the physical work of description, measurement, etc., so all we had to do was examine for any changes since then (e.g. replacement of the shop-front, new cold-room or loading bay, improved staff facilities), take fresh photographs, check the key plan and make a spot-estimate of rental value; but in Scotland a great deal of ground had to be covered and I could not get though more than perhaps eight inspections a day around Glasgow or as few as only two or three in the Highlands. At that rate it was obviously impossible for me to get through the whole lot single-handed so Mr Stephens offered to give me a hand with the remotest: tossing a coin to decide whether he would do the handful on Orkney and Shetland or those on the Outer Hebrides. He won the former, leaving me with the latter.

Hebridean Misadventure

Never having visited the Outer Isles in my life, and previous reports for some forgotten reason being of no assistance as to valuations, I had to do some homework and plan carefully. So I consulted the Scottish Law List to identify the biggest firm of solicitors-cum-estate-agents in Stornoway, got through by telephone to the partner dealing with business premises (although it sounded as if he and the others all did everything) and arranged that he would meet me off the boat and I would buy him lunch in exchange for his views on the four properties concerned. It went well; he was most agreeable and informative, familiar with the subjects and with capital values. "They are worth around £6,000", he advised, which sounded far too low; especially after a quick tour the next day which revealed that they were general stores, much more than grocers, enjoying a virtual monopoly in each centre. But when I called back to take my leave he was insistent, and of course no comparable evidence of market values existed. So, on the return journey I wrote up my inspections and put the poorest property down at £4,000, the best at £8,000 and the other two somewhere in between.

When Stephens and I had completed and gathered together all the Scottish 600 or thereby, they were submitted to Mr Williamson who in turn collected all 3,000 plus, still in draft form, and forwarded to the estates director of Allied Suppliers, Malcolm Cooper, to check for any obvious errors before authorizing production of the full report. A week later Stephens ordered me to accompany him to a meeting as some figures of mine had been queried. There I was confronted by all H&B's retail property partners presided over by the dreaded Williamson, who challenged my Hebridean valuations, whereupon I confessed my source and admitted having felt the figures were far too low. "Too low, you idiot! They are far too high – go back to your lawyer friend and think again!" Which I did, explaining how I had spread the valuations within his brackets, whereupon he exclaimed: "No, no, I meant about £6,000 for the lot!" So each commanded a capital value of anything from a thousand to fifteen hundred pounds. He was quite right, because the physical value of the sites and buildings was negligible: what we were valuing was little more than goodwill – the relics of the legacies of William Lever ("the Soapman") and the great Glaswegian Thomas Lipton. The Outer Isles were very depressed then; crofting communities with few social services, hardly any other business, tourism still embryonic, and very limited accessibility; whereas now several of those locations are flourishing thanks to tourism and enterprising immigrant retailers.

Bear in mind, too, that our prescribed method of valuation was occasionally a straitjacket that did not fit local market conditions. For the procedure – necessary to ensure consistency across such a huge group exercise – was to estimate a notional market rental value, deduct the feu duty and any other 'ground annuals' to arrive at net rental income and then apply an estimated and equally notional 'years' purchase' factor to reflect the yield required by an investor, producing the notional investment value of the property. But this particular case exposed the fallacy of this formula, for an imaginary investor acquiring a property producing a net rental income of say £30 per annum secured by the Allied Suppliers covenant would have been happy at that time with a comparatively low yield of say 5% resulting in a capital value of £600; but in the absence of Allied Suppliers the property would have been occupied by a private trader – a ship's chandler or corn merchant or tractor repairer – from whom this fictitious investor would have required an unrealistic return of say 16% per annum resulting in a capital value of £187.50. Same property but less than one third of the value; hence the local lawyer's low valuations, with which H&B concurred, to reflect the increasing risk (indeed likelihood) that Allied Suppliers would eventually quit. An extreme case but interesting – and an object lesson for me. I grew accustomed thereafter to my colleagues' jibes: "Off to the Hebrides for your holidays this summer-Easter-Christmas, Vivian?"

Another widely dispersed group revaluation was Allied Bakeries, which led to rapid consolidation at the retail end of the bakery industry and vertical integration above it, from the cereal production end through manufacturing and distribution, to create empires such as Garfield Weston's Associated British

Foods, a process with which H&B were closely involved. Again, local loyalties across the country – such as George Strathdee and Mitchell & Muill in Aberdeen, the several old brands within the City Bakeries group in Glasgow – disappeared overnight. Luckily, the Allied Bakeries' revaluation did not include any outlets in the Western Isles!

Another interesting exercise at which H&B excelled was 'financing out' a big store of which the retailer still retained the 'heritage' (freehold) in order to release capital value. This is a very common and far more sophisticated technique today, but we were pioneering it then – evolving alongside 'sale and lease-back'. Hugh Fraser, typically, having bought local department stores throughout Scotland and the North of England with their freehold or very long leasehold titles which were often worth more themselves than what he had paid for the company, could raise cash by this means, selling the investment to an insurance company or pension fund, in return for paying a rent which represented a much lower rate than what he would have had to pay by borrowing in the money market.

I particularly recollect such a deal involving Binns department store (part of a Sunderland-based chain acquired by Fraser) at the west end of Princes Street in Edinburgh, which H&B sold to the Legal & General for a sum that neatly covered what Fraser wanted, which must have been c.£500,000. The lease-back was for a term of 99 years at a rent that was subject to review only after 33 and 66 years, whereas now a rent fixed for longer than 10 years would be unthinkable, such has been the devastation wrought by inflation during the last quarter of the last century. So typically today, even for a large store, a lease might be granted for say 40 years subject to review every 5 years; although I can never understand why for stand-alone department stores – and supermarkets, too – far greater use is not made of turnover rents, whereby a percentage of gross sales is paid as rent, which is perfectly feasible and foolproof with electronic tills, and creates a real sense of partnership between lessor and lessee.

Old Hugh Fraser, who liked to give his occupation as 'draper', was celebrated for conducting meetings over breakfast almost every day, extending for a couple of hours to accommodate a series of guests or co-directors, in a dining-room within his executive suite entered from Argyll Arcade off Buchanan Street in Glasgow, at a round table covered by an exquisite lace cloth with matching place-mats and napkins, at which his guests were invited to sit to partake of a continuous buffet served by immaculate waitresses; but it was an unnerving experience, as our nonchalant host was well aware, because confidential discussion was impeded by the presence of others who were familiar to him but never introduced as they came and went, conferring on him a psychological advantage that was magnified by a visitor's (especially a newcomer's) constant terror, while trying to present a case, of spilling fruit juice or knocking over a crystal glass onto that palatial table. He was the ring-master, cracking the whip, while we walked tightropes and jumped through hoops. He was the only one of the great retail tycoons with whom I dealt personally: his knowledge of detail was incredible, but it proved a grave defect in executive style because he could not delegate once the group grew too big for him to manage.

Consequently, having become Britain's biggest department store operator by acquiring Harrod's, ennobled as Lord Fraser of Allander and diversified by creating Scottish & Universal Investments as well as developing the Aviemore winter sports resort, he lost control, and died in 1966 at the age of only 63. The 'Woolworth' lesson, once again: stick to what you excel in. He had lost heart too, because his son ('Young Hugh') could not possibly emulate that level of enterprise and died aged only 54 in 1987.

Within town centres themselves, wholesale changes inevitably followed the birth of self-service retailing and of credit cards, coupled with expansion of car-ownership. In Edinburgh's renowned Princes Street, for example, only sixty years ago those shops and department stores to the West of The Mound/Hanover Street closed on Wednesday and Saturday afternoons, as they concentrated on the traditional 'carriage trade', their leisured customers running credit accounts; whereas the Eastern half (extending up the Bridges and down Leith Walk) was cash trade for the lower classes. That segregation (necessary prior to credit cards) dissolved within the course of the 1960s; a dissolution accelerated by the demise of the half dozen gentlemen's clubs owning superb Victorian buildings at close intervals along that Western stretch, which had become anachronisms in post-war, classless society, and so were acquired and brutally redeveloped to accommodate large retail stores.

But the Edinburgh planners then had no idea what revolutions were taking place in the outside world. Another cause of this transformation, which turned Princes Street and many other formerly gracious shopping promenades throughout the country into poor imitations of Oxford Street, was closure of the several large tea-rooms and traditional eating places (some even multi-storey) along the length of the street, which had catered for families in town as well as for tourists – while public houses were banished to Rose Street, the narrow thoroughfare behind, because in that puritanical society eating and drinking had to be strictly segregated.

My own usual point of arrival and departure on Scottish trips, however, was Glasgow. I had got into a routine of more or less alternating a week in the office and a week "on safari" as Stephens called it. We kept a car in a big garage, Henderson's in Cambridge Street just North of Sauchiehall Street. I always travelled up by railway sleeper from Euston to arrive early in the morning, when the mechanic, whom I telephoned the day before, would have it ready for the road. It was a Morris Oxford, with the same body as those still used fifty years later as taxis on the tumultuous streets of India. The elderly mechanic who became a friend had joined the business as a boy forty years ago, in 1918, when his first job was mucking out stables, before horses were finally put out to grass. By 1960 I had heard through local associates that the business was being sold to a property company for redevelopment as an office block, which was news that he had picked up as a rumour and challenged me to confirm, which I tried to do gently, but he was inconsolable: "I wouldn't have started work here if I'd known it was a temporary job!"

5 ABUNDANCE

So every other week I drove vast distances round and through towns all over Scotland, becoming familiar with details of almost all of the gradually diminishing number of privately owned retail premises – from corner shops in key locations to family-owned department stores – on every High Street and Main Street, as well as with local customs that affected retailing. For within city and major town centres, despite enjoying a monopoly of shopping provision – since supermarkets were barely heard of – it was severely restricted by prohibition of Sunday trading, strictly enforced in Presbyterian Scotland, and further restricted by midweek 'early closing' – which meant that everywhere was shut on a Tuesday or Wednesday or Thursday afternoon, often as well as on Saturday afternoon, according to local tradition – and even further restricted by 'Trades Holidays' which were celebrated by every part of the country on peculiar days of the year, all of which I had to make a careful note of and continually bear in mind, as it was possible to conduct a grand tour from Kelso to Wick over a period of weeks and never find a shop open!

For all these reasons, Scotland was ripe and wide open for the retail revolution to come – the forerunner of the consumerist society. In retrospect I am not proud of my small part in pioneering it, for I lament that parochial, undemanding style of life, but the change was inevitable. Certainly, the exploration and whole process of familiarisation with what was still a delightfully diversified country was most exciting. Traffic was light, urban centres were uncluttered and there were no parking meters.

But at the end of each year the firm's cars were all changed, which meant that three times in my term I had to end a trip by bringing it down from Glasgow to London – in the depth of winter and driving through every town *en route* – a whole day's journey. More than once in thick fog I had to climb fingerposts to read directions. So throughout the rest of the year the only way to travel between London and Scotland was in a railway sleeping-car. Flying was not really an alternative as short-haul services were scarce and rudimentary. Gatwick was just about to open but barely accessible, Heathrow could be reached only by bus from the makeshift terminal on the Earl's Court Road (or by highway robbers called taxi-drivers), while the West of Scotland was served by a runway (flying Dakotas, as I recall) at Renfrew Airport, precursor to Abbotsinch which was precursor to Glasgow International; and the East by a cute little aerodrome at Turnhouse, adapted from an RAF base which had been the home of a famous Spitfire squadron.

'Sleepers', however, were super! Two trains travelled each way six nights a week. I would be asked by the booking clerk "Early or Late?" – corresponding with the two sittings for breakfast in the sumptuous dining car – for which there was plenty of time because steam-trains were much slower, so the journey took all night. On the earlier, a stroll into the dining car as the train laboured up to Shap summit and breakfast finished rolling into Carlisle; on the later, porridge was ready in good time to follow with kippers, toast and coffee before Glasgow. On one memorable morning, the train shuddered to a halt just over Shap and stood there panting, just as we had all taken our seats; then we saw a steward, in his smart uniform (white cut-away jacket with bass buttons and gold epaulettes) leap down to the track from a door directly facing a short track down which he ran to some farm buildings, swinging a large milk churn with which, brimming over, he staggered back a few minutes later, when he was hauled back into the carriage and without a moment's delay the milk, still foaming, was poured into jugs and served with our porridge, to hurrahs from all present.

The sleeping compartments were splendid, with polished wood veneer panelling, solid brass fittings and windows one could open. A little enamel plaque set at eye-level bearing the legend: "a linen drugget will be found on the luggage rack to stand upon when dressing and undressing". Drugget sounds illegal but it was a small carpet; though I always wondered how one was supposed to stand on the luggage rack while dressing and undressing simultaneously.

As if we were embarking on a transatlantic ocean liner, names of all passengers were posted on lists displayed on boards mounted on the station platform for leisurely scrutiny while porters took any heavy luggage into the guard's van. Second-class were printed in type-face half the size of that for first-class, bracketed to correspond with their upper & lower bunks. Thursday nights at Euston featured dozens of MPs heading home, while on August 11th (the eve of the 'Glorious Twelfth' – the start of the grouse-shooting season) the lists read like pages from Burke's Peerage or Debrett. But the real fun was identifying the obviously false names, not just the numerous Mr & Mrs Smith's but the more subtly fictitious ones. For society then was not obsessed with ID and security checks, there were no credit cards or internet, and half of the tickets were paid for in cash, so people could give whatever names they chose, the only difficulty being to remember one's assumed name in the morning. Travel then, even in Britain, was still something of an adventure.

In more remote regions, many families remained immobile for

generations. I once arrived for a meeting by appointment at the offices of a leading firm of solicitors in Inverness. The partner concerned was out and his secretary seemed agitated, while serving me tea and apologizing for the delay, assuring me he would be back soon. Eventually he arrived, very excited, explaining that he had been to Aberdeen. The pleasantries were exhausted before I realized that the significance of his announcement was that he had never been there before! Part of the reason for that otherwise incredible revelation was that the two cities were capitals of different worlds; the domain of Inverness lawyers covering the Northern and Western counties while that of their Aberdeen colleagues the Grampian region and the coast. He must have had to visit Edinburgh occasionally to attend the High Court or Court of Session, and probably Glasgow too for meetings at head offices of some West Highland clients, but could easily have gone through life without ever setting foot in Aberdeen.

Other than the Hebridean misadventure, my two most embarrassing incidents were both bound, by the operation of Murphy's Law, to concern Mr Hemens himself. One, very shortly after I had taken over Scotland, was in preparation for a 'state visit' to Glasgow, though why I cannot recall – I suspect it was for an early look at plans for the new district centres at Easterhouse, Castlemilk and Drumchapel, or for the New Town at East Kilbride. I was instructed to book him into a city centre hotel for one night, but soon discovered that for some reason (apart from the chronic shortage of first-class hotel accommodation generally) Glasgow was completely full. Persevering, I was relieved eventually to get him a bed at the impressive-sounding Great Eastern Hotel on Duke Street, although a little disconcerted by the less-than-professional tone of the receptionist's greeting: "Wha' dya wan'?" Mercifully, I was informed just in time by a friend in Glasgow that the Great Eastern was a doss-house, where new arrivals were handed a blanket and no room key! Instead, a solicitor friend managed to get him into the Western Club. Even more mercifully, this never became public knowledge, although it did gain currency in Glasgow property circles for a while – "Where are you staying tonight, Vivian, the Great Eastern?"

The other *faux-pas* also arose from a 'state visit', this time Dundee, where the great man was to meet the Lord Provost (Mayor) in connection with the proposed redevelopment of the Overgate in the city centre, for which H&B was acting on behalf of the nominated developer, Ravenseft, a subsidiary of what became the mighty Land Securities Investment Trust, one of the largest property companies in the world. This was the first major central area redevelopment project in Scotland. I was instructed to hire a car and driver for a few hours to tour the city and ferry him between railway station and the City Chambers. The driver was to be particularly directed to proceed very slowly so that the great man could take a close look at the buildings. Following his return to London, he regaled the partners with accounts of the wonderful reception he was accorded, not just by Civic heads but by people in the streets. "They all took off their hats and bowed their heads", he exclaimed, bellowing with laughter. When this filtered down to my level, I realized that unwittingly I had hired a 'following' car, for a funeral cortege, with seating for six and a roof so high that even such a big man as him could step in without bending down. So that did no harm, except towards Christmas when planning the next trip after which I had to bring the car back from Glasgow. "Are you swapping the Morris Oxford for a brand new funeral car, Vivian?"

The Overgate

Redevelopment of the Overgate in Dundee, a designated Comprehensive Development Area (which conferred certain powers of compulsory purchase on the promoting local authority), was entrusted following a limited competition to Ravenseft, the provincial development arm of the mighty Land Securities Investment Trust. Not many companies had the skills or resources to undertake such a complex project then and, of those few, hardly any were sufficiently interested in Scotland. Neither my boss Mr Stephens nor my predecessor Maclean had much understanding of central area redevelopment – and I had no experience whatever – yet here we were, presuming to advise a major national developer in consultation with the city Council. We were (to use a favourite cliché of the time) "flying by the seat of our pants". Astonishingly, on 16 October 1958, within two months of starting work in Scotland (and barely five years after arriving in London), I had to represent not only the firm but also the developer at a mass meeting of affected traders held in the Chamber of Commerce Hall, appearing entirely on my own, to explain the plans and programme and answer questions. Luckily it was in the evening, affording the architects a couple of hours in the afternoon to give me a rudimentary briefing.

The reports by 'The Dundee Courier' and 'Glasgow Herald' the following day were exceedingly kind to me, but only because the reporters knew even less than I and in their innocence were in awe of the whole project – and of course wanting it to happen – therefore swallowing whole the assurances and undertakings that I gave to the meeting. The ingenuousness of all concerned is illustrated by the absence from the reports of any reference to Ravenseft – or even to a developer – but merely to me as representative of H&B "acting on behalf of the promoting finance group", because they were unaware of the existence of development companies.

Back in London I learnt that Hemens himself had sent a memo round the partners explaining why, in such an emergency, I could not be given any support, but assuring them that by all accounts I had acquitted myself well. This was my epiphany: having tasted blood, I wanted more. Working on new developments was much more interesting than dealing in old shops.

Yet, ironically, that scheme never materialized: for having won the competition, Ravenseft lost the prize! This reversal arose from a falling out between the principal and local architects whom Ravenseft had jointly engaged. They were both Mancunians and family friends: John Beardshaw knew Ravenseft and had an established practice based in Manchester, whereas Ian Burke had worked as an Admiralty architect through the war, latterly based in Dundee where he decided to stay, lecturing at the city's College of Art. When commissioned by Ravenseft to prepare a scheme for the Overgate competition, Beardshaw – ignorant of Scotland – naturally enlisted Burke's assistance. So they were successful, but what Beardshaw did not realize was that Burke considered his design archaic and unimaginative, which it certainly was. It was as conventional as those developments at Notting Hill Gate and Swiss Cottage mentioned earlier, simply replacing old with new on the existing vehicular street pattern. Burke could see a golden chance to set himself up with his own practice by producing a far more advanced alternative based on a pedestrian precinct, showed his sketches in confidence to my predecessor Maclean at Bernard Thorpe & Partners in Edinburgh (a firm later absorbed into DTZ) who knew the background and in turn talked to new friends at the Murrayfield Real Estate Company, an aggressive developer based in London but by an historical accident registered in Edinburgh as a public company (originally a land-feuing company) and keen to capitalize on this connection.

So Murrayfield grasped the opportunity, urging Burke to produce his modern concept and show it to his friends on the Council, which promptly adopted it, severing relations with Beardshaw and Ravenseft, both of whom were understandably enraged. Beardshaw was embittered at a personal level, lodging a formal complaint of gross professional misconduct against Burke with the RIBA, which resulted merely in a reprimand of no consequence, while

Ravenseft contemplated taking legal action against the Council but thought better of it, so was left to pay all of Beardshaw's and H&B's abortive fees. It was as if, after a brilliant dress-rehearsal and rave reviews, the show was cancelled on the eve of first night! If only Burke could have confided in Beardshaw and convinced him, or conversely, if Burke had remained loyal to colleague and client, the development of Dundee city centre would have taken an entirely different course.

But Healey & Baker remained totally detached from the ensuing drama, although somewhat irked by both Bernard Thorpe & Partners and Murrayfield. This briefest-ever debut in the world of urban redevelopment, catapulted in and straight out again, left me tantalized and intrigued. But I soon got to know the rapidly expanding Murrayfield team, as an English provincial colleague at H&B, Robin Goble, had quit and (after a year working for Victor Kempner, another wealthy solo investor/dealer like Archie Sherman) had just joined Murrayfield, while the other Robin, my friend Trueblood, was about to follow.

I also made friends with Ian Burke and with another College of Art lecturer, Hugh Martin, with whom he set up in partnership as Ian Burke Martin & Partners on the strength of winning the Overgate project. Indeed, Burke and I became the closest of companions and colleagues for the next thirty-odd years until he died, when I composed his obituary for 'The Scotsman'. During our early acquaintance he rather absent-mindedly bought a beautiful Victorian mock-baronial castle, Dalnaglar, in Highland Perthshire, complete with lodge, forestry, fishing rights, etc., by auction at Thomas Love's in Perth, which he had attended only because of a possible interest in some paintings that were included in the contents, all of which – the entire inventory – had been sold before the final lots came up, comprising the castle itself and everything that went with it, by which time hardly anybody was left in the room. The dealers had departed – Thomas Love's were fine art and furniture specialists with little expertise in country houses – so Burke stayed on out of architectural curiosity and it was knocked down to him at what he knew, without ever seeing the place but solely from local knowledge and frantic perusal of the catalogue, was a fraction of its value; as was proved within months when, having sold off the forestry, fishing rights and whatever else, he was left with the castle and 'policies' (surrounding grounds) for a trifling outlay. My young family and I took refuge there more than once towards the end of touring holidays in the far North when, in those pre-credit card days, we invariably ran out of money.

After Murrayfield's break-through, an army of developers from the South invaded Scotland, for whom I found myself acting as a chief scout.

Consequently, devoting an increasing amount of my time and effort to investigating and pursuing possible development opportunities, mostly long-term exercises and mostly abortive – since, out of every five potential projects two would prove a waste of time and one I would lose to a competitor, leaving two successes at best – more and more of my regular agency and valuation work with existing stocks of property had to be delegated to a newly recruited assistant.

Even successes proved an embarrassment, because every regular client of the firm who was competent in this sector and prospectively interested in Scotland expected first refusal. Mr Stephens or any of the senior partners could tell me, "Linacre, I hear you are looking into a possible shopping development in Falkirk: well, you'll be pleased to know I've got a client for you; it's Whitehall Wigwams", to which I'd reply, "Thank you, Sir, that makes three, because the local Councillors whisper that to win planning permission I'd better take it to West Lothian Water Closets, while our old client Mega-Babel plc have just notified their presumption that I was acting for them." This sort of situation was becoming intolerably invidious.

Three Wise Men

One way to escape this quandary unobtrusively was by cultivating discreet Scottish entrepreneurs, of whom there were three in Glasgow who all shunned publicity, whom I could trust absolutely and whose advice I valued. All were Jewish, two of them solicitors with vast private interests in property and commerce, the other an astute property dealer and investor, celebrated within the confines of our professional circles but indifferent to anything beyond his comprehension or personal control. The two lawyers were Harold Dykes and Alex Stone, the property professional Isadore Walton. All were towering personalities, the closest of friends, never risking unnecessary competition yet never working together.

Harold Dykes was a handsome, entertaining and immensely enterprising operator, who executed a classic manoeuvre with a scheme that I devised in Falkirk at the Callendar Riggs end of the High Street, comprising some forty shops, an hotel, etc., and underground car-park. 'The Falkirk Herald' of 30 April 1960 reported on a press conference during a lunch held on the 25th, at which he presided, narrating the two years history of the project and quoting the total cost of the development as £600,000. The other speakers were the Provost William Leishman, Police Judge James Paterson (Convener of the

Council's Planning Committee), the architect Baron Bercott and myself. The whole site had been assembled in phases until finally assigned to the Council in return for a long Ground Lease back to Mr Dykes' specially formed Falkirk Development Company.

Now the salient benefit of having as one's developer client an *ad hoc* property company owned by one's solicitor is that decisions are taken instantly and the legal documentation is framed and drafted to suit the objectives of the client without disclosure by way of correspondence. There is no question of any conflict of interest between lawyer and client: on the contrary, their interests are identical. But the disadvantage from my own point of view was that I had no idea of what my client had in mind; nor did the Town Clerk (or Depute) as the Council's solicitor, who in any event did not possess anything like Mr Dykes' expertise. So it came as a complete surprise when I learnt a few months later that my client had (perfectly legitimately) exploited the omission from the Ground Lease of any prohibition against creating a Sub-Lease (Ground Underlease) by doing precisely that; simply sub-letting the whole site with the benefit of the planning consents and all the progress to date, to a major development company, presumably at a greatly enhanced ground rent (or with equity participation – I never learnt the terms), leaving him with an effortless, substantial, and virtually perpetual profit income.

I doubt if such a coup had been accomplished before – or has been since! Incidentally, the agent acting for the other development company, who had quietly negotiated the deal with Dykes, was yet another ex-colleague from H&B, Peter Chuck, who had quit to assume charge of Bernard Thorpe & Partners in Scotland (after Maclean had moved on to set up his own practice in Glasgow) and who later became Godfather to my youngest son.

The other well-disposed, easily accessible and highly resourceful lawyer was Alex Stone, an immensely cultured, brilliant intellectual and a very rare human being. He died aged 91 in 1998, but thirty-odd years earlier I could not have predicted what a legend Sir Alexander Stone was to become; the greatest benefactor of Glasgow University of our times, who endowed a chair in Commercial Law, a Lectureship in Rhetoric, a Lectureship in Bibliophily, the Alexander Stone Building at Garscube for the Departments of Medical Oncology and Microbiology, the Alexander Stone Building for the School of Law – the list continues – yet he was the soul of humility. He had a lovely wry sense of humour, informing me that his surname was adopted by his father as an immigrant from Estonia, just as he told me that the original Montague Burton had assumed that name because in a thick fog on travelling North by train from

London he had got off at Burton-on-Trent thinking he had reached Leeds, the centre of the clothes manufacturing industry, but I never knew whether or not to believe him.

For such was his sense of humour that he enjoyed introducing himself as the Chairman of the BBC and of KLM; disclosing later that the former was a small merchant bank ("my funkhole") off Hanover Square called the British Bank of Commerce (he told me that the Earl of Harewood was on the Board but again that may have been a tease) while of course the latter was not the Royal Dutch Airline but the Kirkcaldy Linoleum Market – the retail end of what once was an important manufacturing industry. As late as 1980 at the age of 73 he founded a second merchant bank in Renfield Street, Glasgow, called Combined Capital Ltd, but heaven alone knows why he bothered. And somehow he managed to find time to collect nineteenth century books, specializing in the byways of English and Scottish literature – hence the bibliophily. We effected several nice transactions in retail property and development projects, but all with private clients rather than with any of his own companies – though that was perhaps a fine distinction. Roman law was his passion, and its influence on Scots law. His was one of the two or three finest minds I have ever encountered.

The third local ally, Isadore Walton, was Glasgow's first home-grown property investor and developer to join the premier league. His vehicle, Scottish Metropolitan Property PLC, grew out of the small St. Mungo Property Company, the acquisition of which was just being completed by David Stephens when I started working for him. Because Glasgow's inner suburbs consisted of clearly defined districts with distinct characters and strong loyalties and were centred on stretches of main streets radiating in all directions from the city centre, lined with densely populated tenements where half the population still lived, and also because the ground floors of these tenements in the main street blocks all consisted of small shops which were almost always individually owned (having been sold off long ago, whether or not the flats above were still rented), for all these reasons there was a brisk trade in these shops – a regular turnover with recognized levels of value and a steady demand for any vacancies.

But Walton turned them into an investment commodity, quickly building up an impressive portfolio with the security of a wide spread throughout these districts. In an unguarded moment he explained the *modus operandi*: borrow say £10,000 at 6% interest to buy a shop, annual cost £600;

let it to a good tenant ("first-class covenant") at a rent of £1,000, exclusive of rates on a full repairing & insuring lease, to show a 10% return; profit income £400 per annum. Or, on a capital basis: the created investment on a 6% yield is worth £16,666 gross, say £15,000 after H&B's fees and legals, producing a profit of no less than 50%. To set up that quality of operation, we certainly earned our fees, but even at only 25% profit he did not complain! My contemporaries assured me that there was an Izzy Walton or several mini-Izzies in every major English city too.

That class of business, his staple diet in the early days, could not continue much longer in Glasgow because those inner-suburban districts based on high densities of tenements declined severely or even disappeared as a result of (a) the Council's massive slum demolition programme (funded by Central Government – the most extensive such operation in Europe) covering 29 Comprehensive Development Areas of which 16 were also to clear a huge belt for construction of a new Ring Road around the entire central area; (b) dispersal of the displaced population to brand new outer suburban districts such as Drumchapel, Castlemilk and Easterhouse (to live in high-rise flats, condemned to live as life-tenants of the Council which lacked any experience or expertise in the necessary management and maintenance, and in soulless environs lacking any community facilities); and (c) the arrival of multiple retailers which wanted larger standard shop units, loading bays, car-parking and longer leases; and (d) the extent to which Walton himself had outgrown that rudimentary class of property investment. For he was becoming far more ambitious in class and scale of business, both on the ground and at the corporate level.

But he never understood property development – it was too unpredictable, too difficult to control over the life-span of a project. After my first year in Scotland we lost touch, but fifteen years later renewed contact when I was the first Group Property Manager of Trusthouse Forte, based in Grosvenor House on Park Lane, two years after the merger of Forte and Trust Houses.

It is infuriating to a property professional that when two large companies not primarily in property – e.g. in manufacturing or service industries – propose to amalgamate their first priority is invariably to take care of the respective boards of directors, their second to pacify the shareholders, their third to rationalize their areas of activity and identify economies, and only their fourth and final objective is to combine respective estate management functions – often long after the new executive structures and line management regimes have bedded in. Management of any large company's or institution's property – both to maximize as an asset and for performance as part of the organisation's activities – is usually the Cinderella among service departments, because those in charge don't understand it.

One end of the Grosvenor House complex comprised a block of luxurious service flats, mostly let long-term to regular visitors, one of whom was 'Izzy' Walton who would, if he had nothing better to do, ring my office to invite me to visit his flat for drinks with him and his wife and a chat about property in Scotland. What appealed to him especially was that his flat, in the heart of the empire ruled by Forte, was No. 40 – the personalized car numberplate mentality.

But he was a monumental figure in the history of Scottish real estate. Without the qualifications of Dykes or Stone, he succeeded by sheer dedication and industry. Also, unlike Dykes, who was all too well aware of the anti-Semitic prejudice which was still rife (even institutionalized) in Glasgow fifty years ago but who charmed his way round it, and unlike Stone who was far too superior culturally to pay it any attention, Walton was highly sensitive to it. As I recall, a son of his was the first Jewish broker to be admitted to the Glasgow Stock Exchange – incredible now but an important achievement then.

M & S

My biggest deal and most noteworthy development scheme by 1960 was to identify, assemble and secure planning permission for the development of Marks & Spencer's first store in Perth, the ancient capital city of Scotland, where H&B had been under pressure to secure a suitable site since before David Stephens' time. For so long M&S had only three stores in the whole of Scotland; in Glasgow, Edinburgh and Aberdeen. Their expansionist priorities were Perth (overdue and most urgent), Dunfermline (urgent after Perth to fit in geographically), then Inverness, Dumfries, Stirling and Ayr (whenever). Healey & Baker were pursuing comparable priorities throughout the English regions, as I learnt from my colleagues.

The Perth opportunity arose from the Council's own scheme for redevelopment of derelict premises and yards covering a land-locked area behind the High Street with access from an ancient street called Meal Vennel down one side and from South Street at the rear, to form what it called the Meal Vennel Precinct, consisting of numerous small shop units, all facing inwards, onto an open square, with office suites on one or two upper floors. I saw that if (a) we could acquire from the Council the three units planned to form a section of the North side of this square, so as to constitute the back end of a store with ample depth from the High Street, and if (b) the corresponding half-dozen existing small shops on the South side of the High Street could also be acquired to afford an adequate frontage; then the rear boundaries of the two blocks would meet and they could be combined to create a roughly rectangular site for redevelopment.

So I proceeded with utmost stealth, ensuring that the High Street proprietors learnt nothing of my dealings with the Council while the Council did not suspect that I wanted more than to lease those three units in the Precinct. But the High Street proprietors, once I had persuaded each of them in principle to agree to sell, inevitably compared notes and joined forces, appointing a leading Perth surveyor, James King, to act for them collectively. He was very sound professionally and we became friends, so I could confidentially explain my plans, which he swore would not be leaked to the Council or District Valuer; but I did not disclose my client's identity, which so far as he was concerned could have been any one of several major store groups.

A walk-through store such as this, with a second frontage at the rear, was then known as an arcade store, while Woolworths and others that sold bits of everything were known as 'bazaar stores'; whereas M&S and their rivals Littlewoods, specializing in clothes (and food later) but still trading on only one or two floors, were known as 'variety stores': all as distinct from department stores which also specialized in furniture and household goods but could sell almost anything and traded on as many floors as suited their range and location.

James King was immensely tall, and whenever we met to negotiate he would suggest that we step outside his office to cross Atholl Place onto a public park called the North Inch (meaning 'island') to conduct our dialogue while enjoying a brisk walk. So he would stride out while I (half a foot shorter) trotted alongside him. But we succeeded in striking a bargain. Luckily, all the properties but one were owner-occupied, the exception being an annual tenant whom we undertook to compensate generously. I congratulated myself on beating King down from his valuation of say £150,000 for the lot to say £130,000 on which we shook hands, while I turned attention to the Council officials to whom I then disclosed our real intentions, explaining why my client needed to purchase that block of three notional Meal Vennel units outright instead of merely leasing them. The officials, thrilled at the prospect of the arrival of M&S, were most cooperative, but it proved difficult to convince the District Valuer that the glamorous status of the prospective purchaser did not necessarily enhance the value of the site to be acquired. While that was progressing I appointed local architects – McKillop & Mackintosh, marvellous Highland gentlemen – to prepare and pursue a planning application, realizing that a London firm was bound to be brought in to design the new store and supervise the project. I meanwhile rounded off the main frontage by the purchase of one more shop on the High Street-Meal Vennel corner from Kidds the old-established Dundee bakers.

Mighty pleased with myself once all this was tied up, I was not surprised to receive a summons to the office of A E F Giffard, Estates Director of M&S at Head Office in Baker Street – to be presented with a medal, or so I presumed. (Lots of initials seemed a pre-requisite to his job; his successor, with whom I worked closely ten years later, was J A E H White.) But, having waded through the deep pile carpet from his office door to stand in front of his massive desk, behind which he (shorter than I) was ostentatiously busy, I waited vainly for an invitation to be seated, until he eventually looked up and barked: "Oh, yes, Linacre, you're the genius who nearly lost us the once-in-a-generation chance of acquiring a store in Perth, for the sake of saving a paltry £20,000 in site-purchase costs......Good afternoon! Stephens had, with the best of intentions, given him a full report on my negotiations. Giffard was right, of course.

Once the scheme became public knowledge, the populace were delighted but, predictably, the local private drapers, dress shops and outfitters were up in arms, objecting to this monster which threatened to wipe out dozens of private traders that had served Perth so well, etc.; blind to the consequent enlargement of the town's catchment area and shopping population, uplift in property values, huge increase in economic activity and opportunities to trade off M&S by increased specialization. It was ever thus. Meanwhile once certain that planning approval was forthcoming, M&S quickly mopped up the remaining properties on that side of Meal Vennel to fill out the site. Without this busy direct link with the High Street, the Meal Vennel Precinct would have been a back-yard and barely viable; but instead it became the nucleus of what became the St John's Centre, Perth's only shopping mall, into which the Meal Vennel and several other lanes and closes disappeared altogether.

So successful was the M&S store that some twenty years later it had outgrown the site and acquired a stretch on the opposite side of High Street, disposing of its old store to BhS, who traded there for another twenty-odd years until retrenchment in the present recession caused them to sell to Primark who completely rebuilt it. That M&S episode in Perth of more than fifty years ago certainly taught me more and possibly gave even more satisfaction than either of my later successful M&S projects: East Kilbride New Town Centre (mentioned later) or my greatest solo success of later years, the Eastgate Centre in Inverness, undertaken by Vivian Linacre Estates (Inverness) Limited in 1978 following a competition conducted by the Highland Regional Council, in which my two short-listed rivals were Trafalgar House and my Wester Hailes adversary Samuel Properties!

The difference between my first deal with M&S as an agent in Perth and my last as the developer in Inverness was that within that period of just twenty years the market had so far matured that as a result I could presume to give them advice on space requirements and competition. Yet even now, British developers of shopping centres differ from their US, Australian and some European counterparts in that, while carrying out thorough research as developers into planning, traffic, footfall, building costs, services, rental values and yields, they do very little homework on socio-economics, demography and consumer spending from a retailing point of view for presentation to potential tenants.

Meanwhile, around 1960, Richard Ellis and Jones Lang Wootton both opened in Scotland, initially in Glasgow. Competition was hotting up on both the agency and the development fronts. Solo entrepreneur developers were "flying blind" from London, relying on one of the big four firms of agents to navigate and hold their hands, although Healey & Baker, despite its hyper-activity there, was restricted in this role on the ground until opening a Scottish branch office much later.

One of the few of these ambitious explorers who actually came to us at H&B in London for guidance before venturing to the far North was a very young man whom my contemporary Neville Pearson invited me to meet in his office without warning. I later learnt that until a few weeks earlier he had been working in his father's furniture factory ever since leaving school at 15 but now had been told to get out and into property development, so he was doing the rounds of the big firms to find out what they could offer. Neville had nothing available below six figures in Central London so could I help in Scotland?

I mumbled about suggesting a few possibilities for discussion, whereupon our guest asked if I was free for lunch. Anything to miss the usual cheese sandwich, so no question of asking what I would like, never mind telephoning to book, but straight into a taxi down to Jermyn Street and into 'A l'Ecu de France' (as I recall), a restaurant of such opulence as I had never seen, and at one word with the Head Waiter we were shown to one of the best tables. He cannot have been a regular diner there, but that didn't matter; the point was that he had such natural, overwhelming self-assurance – the chutzpah – to get what he wanted. Overawed, I tried frantically to scrape up one or two retail development or dealing prospects for him, one of which – a couple of old shops ripe for redevelopment to form one modern unit at the Southern end of Kirkcaldy High Street I believe he went ahead and bought – but may well have turned for a profit after obtaining the redevelopment planning consent. At all events, he seemed happy enough but soon moved onto bigger things. This was Gerald Ronson, aged just 21.

Glasgow District Centres

Another incentive to my work on new development projects was provided by Glasgow's "Overspill" programme, which was roaring ahead in line with the slum clearances. New District Centres were planned on the outskirts of the city, each requiring a shopping centre, for which competitions were held to choose a developer. Drumchapel to the NW and Castlemilk to the SE were each planned for a population of about 30,000, work starting on both in 1953. But neither the City councillors nor the officials had any idea how to prepare a brief for interested developers nor how to conduct these competitions nor how to assess and adjudicate upon the submitted entries – how, essentially, to reconcile the three criteria: architectural and commercial merits of the scheme design, value of financial bid and quality of funding, experience of the developer and professional team. But we acted in both contests with different clients: Drumchapel with a private developer, which we lost, and Castlemilk, with Ravenseft (who had been our client at Dundee) which H&B won.

The results were stereotypical, exactly as for any massive council housing estates anywhere in Britain, and both doomed to deteriorate in quality of tenants with the deterioration of the environment. Yet the success or failure of the shopping centres largely depended on the quality and management of the housing, which was the essential weakness of the whole system dominated by entrenched Labour councils. For in these districts the Corporation owned the land, was planning authority, sometimes even main building contractor too, through its 'Direct Labour' department, and housing manager for good measure, conferring the power of selecting tenants from the waiting lists; creating an absolute monopoly which was the ideal prescription for pure housing Hell. Experience in factoring hundred-year old tenements that required little more than rent-collecting, emergency repairs and cleaning of common parts, was no qualification for managing high-rise blocks with lifts, central heating, refuse disposal, car-parking, security systems, etc. – not to mention rootless tenants.

Yes, every old industrial city in Britain was obliged to decant people from its slums into new settlements far away from amenities and adequate facilities; but only Glasgow was confronted with the problem on such a vast scale that it needed four District Centres – Pollok to the South and Easterhouse to the East as well as Drumchapel and Castlemilk – each of which was an average-sized town. At all events, that one-off generation of district centres was quickly outmoded by out-of-town supermarkets and retail warehouses and by the ever-rising demands of consumers.

We were also involved in the early New Town centres at Glenrothes, Irvine and East Kilbride (once we managed to find them in the wilds, respectively, of Fife, Ayrshire and Lanarkshire!). One town centre shopping development on which Mr Stephens and I acted was 'The Piazza' in Paisley: it was undistinguished but interesting because it was built on a deck across the White Cart River, giving rise to legal issues of riparian rights for which the authorities had failed to prepare; i.e. the rights relating to the river-banks, originally the land between high and low-water levels; prompting the suggestion that the shop tenants' obligations, instead of the normal 'full repairing and insuring', should be full *riparian* and insuring!

But, as with my predecessors, the travelling between London and Glasgow every other week, and absences from my growing family, as well as the driving all round Scotland like one of the legion of 'commercial travellers' and staying in cheap hotels from one night to the next, all gradually all eroded my enthusiasm. Worse, I suffered a growing sense of grievance over my inadequate level of earnings. The secret salary scales and sacred routine of annual reviews, so carefully drawn up and administered by the partners, could not be disturbed or even questioned; but with a wife and three sons, living in Berkshire, I simply could not manage on the £1,500 p.a. I was then earning.

So in desperation, as Mr Stephens could not intervene, I made a special request to see Mr Hemens himself; rather like Oliver Twist daring to approach the supervisor to ask for more! He listened amiably enough but then told me to go away and produce a monthly household budget to show him at another meeting a few days later. This was a humiliating instruction which nobody would put up with today but I had no alternative, convincing myself that he would not have requested it except with a view to awarding an exceptional increase and that to take such an interest in my domestic affairs demonstrated a rare concern for my future. So I spent hours with my wife drawing up a monthly balance sheet, which unavoidably showed a net loss, or at best a zero surplus for savings and the most meagre allowance for holidays. A special burden was our monthly repayments under hire-purchase agreements (into which almost every young household had to enter in order to acquire furniture, etc. when starting out in married life). So when I ashamedly presented it to Hemens at our next (and last!) meeting, he merely took one look at it and, with his pen, ringed round the sum for hire purchase repayments and pushed it back to me with a masterly "There you are, Linacre, your problem is solved: all you have to do to restore solvency is clear off those hire purchase agreements – and don't buy anything else until you can afford to pay for it!" I knew then that I would not be staying much longer.

Australia

The world suddenly opened up. We could go anywhere. British developers, followed by British firms of surveyors, were already invading France, Belgium and the Netherlands – what their hosts called *'le défi Anglais'*.

But the complete change of direction came about as a result of two major events. The first was my elder brother's emigration to Australia, with wife and three sons, on the maiden voyage of the old 'Oriana' in December 1960 (he became Professor of Climatology at Macquarie University in Sydney). From the earliest news of his plans I naturally started to take a vague interest in the first wave of British surveyors, estate agents who were pioneering the property professions out there. The very first were missionaries from Jones Lang Wootton, a firm I knew very well, which was owned (I believe) by the Taylor family comprising two brothers and their elderly father. The timing was perfect because they had already established a highly successful office in Sydney and were very keen to open others quickly. On a mega-scale, it was not unlike the situation that had first confronted me in Scotland just two years ago! The temptation was irresistible: I arranged an interview with Noel Taylor in their City office, where to my surprise we were joined by both his brother and father. It was immediately obvious that in their minds the only question was how soon I could get out there – Oh yes, and did I think the second office should be in Melbourne or in Canberra, the capital? They even put me in personal touch right away with the partner in charge at Sydney to agree on the answer to that question and settle the domestic arrangements. My wife and I were consumed with excitement and complications.

But then came the second major event. I had confided my tentative interest in Oz to my friend Robin Trueblood, who had joined Murrayfield Real Estate Co. Ltd. a few months earlier, as also had another H&B colleague, Robin Goble. Trueblood in turn confided in Murrayfield's Managing Director, which he ought not to have done but did with the very best intentions, knowing that the company was unhappy with the management of its office in Glasgow and of the projects in Scotland to which it was already committed. So his boss, the mercurial Walter Flack – dispensing with correspondence and secretaries – got straight on the phone and, before I even realized what was happening, had arranged for me to meet him and his deputy Alan Wright in their head office at Neale House, which was not, as it sounds, a modern office block but the proper name of this original, narrow, Regency town-house on St James's Street.

Once again – twice in one month – the interview was almost dreamlike, as if my joining them were a *fait accompli.* A salary augmented by a car and expenses (a substantial perquisite then because of the liberal, indeed lax, tax regime that treated most expenditure on 'subsistence' and 'entertainment of clients' as deductible), plus all costs of relocation to Glasgow – altogether a very seductive package. No more commuting from Sandhurst via Camberley, Victoria and Oxford Circus every day one week alternating with a week of railway sleepers and driving all round Scotland, and no more perpetual worries about money; instead, the opportunity to concentrate on new development projects, for which I had acquired a growing appetite and a real talent, and to learn much more about property finance and the investment market, about which I knew far too little, while working with highly congenial colleagues in both Glasgow and London.

This last consideration mattered considerably, after my isolated life in Scotland with H&B. Addressing one another formally as "Mr Stephens" and "Linacre" was normal in those days, but I did mind very much that it never occurred to him to suggest once in a while that we might pop out for lunch together or for a drink after hours.

So for an agonising week I had three jobs, while H&B remained wholly unaware of my manoeuvrings: until one simple and totally unexpected initiative forced a decision. In the post there arrived from Murrayfield's lawyers in Edinburgh a Service Agreement (contract of employment) ready for me to sign, covering every detail, from use of a company car to a directorship of the Scottish subsidiary, from medical insurance to expenses accounting – tailor-made very specifically to suit my circumstances yet produced as the finished article within a matter of days, dispensing with drafts and laborious consultation.

I was so overwhelmed by this exceptional personal consideration and lightning performance that, in a daze, I signed and returned it. (H&B had always refused solicitations from senior staff for some form of Service Agreement, the proprietors determined to retain absolute control – if only they had not been so obdurate!) They arrival of this document left me with two urgent and equally unpleasant tasks, quite apart from planning the family's emigration. There is little doubt that if, just a week earlier, Jones Lang Wootton had sent me a comprehensive Service Agreement and *modus operandi*, I would have signed it; and the whole of my own and my family's future - these last fifty years plus whatever lies ahead – would have been entirely different. But Walter Flack's precipitate, aggressive tactics were not the Taylors' style. For they were gentlemen, naturally assuming that their Sydney partner and I would work everything out between us, for a contract to be drawn up once full agreement had been reached. Consequently, they were aghast at both Flack's buccaneering methods and – as they saw it – my betrayal.

I may have made a cosmic blunder by opting instead for Glasgow; but we were preoccupied by immediate concerns, chiefly worries about the future of our respective mothers and siblings and about short-term financial security; specifically (it sounds ridiculous looking back but at the time I was at my wits end) the seeming impossibility of surviving financially until we were safely on board. For I could hardly telephone Noel Taylor to say: "You will be pleased to hear, Sir, that all is going well with Sydney and, by the way, could you let me have a sub to keep us going", whereas I had no hesitation in telling Walter Flack that I needed an advance to tide us over, which was readily forthcoming. On such trifling considerations the future of a family can turn.

A grovelling letter of withdrawal to JLW, however embarrassing, was painless; whereas my resignation from H&B, presented to David Stephens face to face, was very painful indeed. He was very bitter, faced yet again with finding a replacement for this problematic department (I was the third H&B deserter to Murrayfield, whose blitzkrieg methods he viewed with distaste, especially in Scotland after the Overgate upset); and also because he felt that my leaving primarily on financial grounds was inadequate – I should not have taken "No" for an answer.

Perhaps he was right on that score, but the others were not my concern. Anyhow, my resolution was reinforced by one of the senior partners who put his head round the door to exclaim: "Linacre, I hear you are leaving – why?" In a surge of anger, knowing it no longer mattered, I suddenly felt impelled to answer: "Because of you, Sir". Whereupon he responded indignantly: "Me? Why? I've never spoken to you in my life" I instantly rejoined: "Precisely!" At which, muttering to himself, he withdrew. Mervyn Orchard-Lisle's son, the illustrious Paul (CBE TD, DL, LLD, etc.) ten years my junior, joined H&B in October that year.

We would no doubt have had a very happy and successful life in Australia, but today, with an ever-growing family here, I can have no regrets. It is ironic that one wonderful consequence of starting with Murrayfield in March 1961, and the family moving into our new Glasgow home two months later, was that the following February our youngest son was born there, who might never have existed had we gone to Oz instead; yet today he is a University Professor – in Australia.

6 ADVENTURE

Having acquired a fair self-esteem as an expert on Scottish commercial property, I quickly moved into my smart office in West George Street and with complete self-assurance pitched straight into the hectic development programme to which it was heavily committed. But within a week or two I suddenly realized to my horror that I was woefully ignorant of the range of skills that are essential to this new discipline of developer: architecture and town planning, quantity surveying and financial planning, structural engineering and building services ('mechanical and electrical') engineering, and project management. My rudimentary qualifications in building construction, valuation and law, were inadequate. So I immersed myself in this range of subjects, praying that my incompetency would not be too brutally or disastrously exposed.

That it was not exposed was not thanks to the plausibility of my performance, but rather to a second shock a few weeks later, when I suddenly realized something else; which was that my fraternity in Glasgow – and indeed the entire commercial property community in Scotland – knew no more than I did, or even less! Moreover, unlike me, they were happily unaware of their deficiencies. Why it had struck me and not them was because (a) I had come up from London, where pioneering skills in retail and office development were already circulating, to a country where they scarcely existed, and (b) I had been working virtually on my own for the last three years, so the impact on me of this primitive market-place was so much sharper upon joining a crowd who collectively were oblivious to it and to the amateurishness of their operations in it.

The remoteness of the Glasgow office from London, the relatively huge sums of money we were involved with, coupled with the liberality of the business expenses regime – the reprehensible spirit of the sixties – all had an undermining effect on discipline. Associates and friends, not only within Glasgow, soon learnt to drop in around noon, when the bar would already be open. Accounts were opened in many top restaurants, while site visits to Dundee or elsewhere – especially involving local politicians – turned into expeditions. Eventually, the chief accountant in London notified us of an imminent two-day visit by his deputy, requesting that we were all available for "consultation" and the books for examination. The immediate reaction from my new colleagues was that we must make sure he enjoys his time with us; so within an hour of his mid-morning arrival we took him out for a monumental lunch that lasted until mid-afternoon, which they all agreed had been a great success. The repercussions accelerated the inevitable.

My professional community in Scotland was meanwhile growing fast. Only weeks before quitting H&B, I had been told by David Stephens to call upon one Kenneth Ryden (a fellow Lancastrian) who had just quit the Ministry of Works along with two other senior surveyors to set up their own practice in Glasgow as Kenneth Ryden & Partners, initially to concentrate on rating and work in the public sector. We met as he was unpacking boxes in an empty office, but of course, it grew into the largest home-grown surveying practice in Scotland, Kenneth Ryden himself becoming a prominent figure nationally. The big firms from London – Jones Lang Wootton, the firm I had nearly joined in Australia (later Jones Lang LaSalle), Richard Ellis (became part of CBRE), followed by Strutt & Parker, Montagu Evans, Edward Erdman *et alia* – soon spread their wings in Scotland. I am the only person to have attended the Scottish office opening parties of both the first two plus both of their 21st or 25th anniversary celebrations. So it was a very good time to get into the mainstream, running the Scottish end of a rapidly growing public property company.

In March' 62, Roddy Maclean departed and I was given charge of the Scottish operation (one year after joining the company) with instructions to run a more rigorous regime, which was soon booming. We had only two chartered surveyors and secretarial staff, yet as at 3rd December 1963 were actively or prospectively engaged in all the projects on this schedule (prepared for a board meeting) that, with a few exceptions as stated, I had introduced and were all completed within less than three years. This is not for the interest of the projects themselves but to illustrate the scale of operation generated.

Aberdeen, Union Street & Huntly Street

Very successfully completed: small supermarket, shops and new YMCA on the upper floors, on prominent corner site previously occupied by two large villas, one of which had been the YMCA's; with lovely granite facade, adjoining the great Music Hall.

Ayr, Dalblair Road/ Alloway Street

Completed not very successfully – done in too much of a rush – featuring a small new hotel in a shopping mall connecting the main street to a back road that did not really lead anywhere.

Bathgate, 21-23 George Street

Successfully completed – small supermarket, shops and (as I recall) offices above – on a site previously occupied by two villas, one owned by a professional firm who were happy to take the cash from a generous valuation for their property with a lease of new offices in its place after a temporary move elsewhere.

Bearsden, 134-138 Drymen Road/ Kirk Road

Successfully completed – small supermarket & shops.

Dundee, Overgate Phases I to III:

Scotland's first large central area redevelopment, as mentioned earlier – which I was closely concerned with but did not initiate and which took far too long because of problems with relocation of existing traders and complex phasing programme -- so was not finished until after my time and was completely redeveloped by new owners c.2000.

Dundee, Macalpine Road

A neighbourhood shopping parade in a large housing estate.

Dunfermline, 12 Guildhall Street/ Canmore Street

Successfully completed – horrible secondary shops in off-pitch town centre.

Edinburgh, Kirkgate, Leith

An open shopping mall prominently located in a slum clearance area – successfully completed but inferior quality design & retailing. Murrayfield assembled the site piecemeal but for a piece owned by the Council, to whom we assigned all our ownerships while they threw in theirs and then granted us a long building lease overall. The opening ceremony was performed by Frank Price (who always reminded me of Edward G Robinson) a main board director, Birmingham city councillor (since 1949 at the age of 27) and head of the Midlands operation, who had a passion for tree-planting to help "green" our cities and teach young people respect for the environment. So a beautiful young maple was brought along, a ceremonial spade acquired, suitably engraved, and Frank delivered a magnificent oration, standing on the specially prepared plot of earth in the centre of the precinct, hemmed in by the mob; but when he turned around for the spade, it had been spirited away, no doubt to be sold a few hours later in a nearby pub. A builder's shovel was hastily substituted and proceedings resumed. The development has been resold and revamped regularly: the basic problem (as with the Gorbals centre (*q.v.*) being simply the poverty of the neighbourhood.

Edinburgh, Nicolson Street Comprehensive Development Area

This was a creature spawned by the monstrous scheme for an Edinburgh ring road – in the notorious era of Professor Colin Buchanan's 'Traffic in Towns', his general solution to the problem being to demolish the towns! Here on the Eastern flank of the Old Town of Edinburgh, wholesale redevelopment was planned alongside the University quarter, so we formed a partnership with the University & the City, but mercifully the mediaeval Old Town and Georgian New Town of Edinburgh were tougher nuts to crack than Liverpool or Birmingham. So this fantasy, at least on the N and E sides, eventually evaporated in face of public outrage at the massive destruction threatened on all sides and stratospheric estimates of the budget for compulsory acquisitions. Here is the preamble to the beautifully printed first Minutes:

"Edinburgh Corporation/ University -- Nicolson Street, etc. Comprehensive Development Area

Minutes of the first Meeting of the Joint Co-ordinating Committee of Edinburgh Corporation, the University of Edinburgh and Murrayfield Real Estate Co. Ltd. held in the University Court Room, Old College, Edinburgh, 1st March 1963. Present: *Edinburgh Corporation* – Councillors A J Ingham and J A Crichton; Messrs E G Glendinning [Depute Town Clerk], T T Hewitson [Chief Planning Officer], G M Dickson [Depute City Engineer] and M M Duncan [Admin.], accompanied by Messrs L Trevor Donaldson [founder & senior partner of Donaldsons the surveyors, consultants to the Corporation] and R A Gammie [partner]; *Edinburgh University* – Professor R N Arnold, Messrs Charles H Stewart [University Principal], R Maxwell Young [University Surveyor] and P Johnson-Marshall [University's architectural and planning consultant – Britain's first globally renowned town planner]; *Murrayfield Real Estate Co. Ltd.* – Messrs R T McPake [Rankin & Reid, our co. secretaries & Scottish solicitors], V T Linacre, I D Burke [architect], A D Lamont [his partner] and L Melville [Gumleys, estate agents]. Councillor Ingham was appointed to the chair.

The Joint Committee had been established to provide machinery, representative of the three interests involved in the promotion of the proposed University – Nicolson Street etc. CDA for joint consultation and advice and for the examination and co-ordination of progress in the development of the scheme. It was accepted that this first meeting must largely be exploratory in character, since the stage had not yet been reached when the necessary information, drawings and so on could be submitted to the

Corporation to allow them to consider in detail, as planning authority, the planning, economic and other relevant implications of the proposals with a view to a statutory comprehensive development area submission to the Secretary of State."

The "other relevant implications" ought to have included the question as to whether there was the faintest possibility of the project ever making progress, but apparently the setting up of the "machinery" was an end in itself. So we had this august assembly of brilliant professionals and public servants, all with the very best of intentions, with ample powers and resources but with no idea of where to go from there – and, of course, with no one party in charge. As always with official bodies, all that mattered was that the machinery was in good order, that there were no defects in the system and that procedures were followed correctly – the perfect recipe for drift and disintegration. Various *ad hoc* meetings of the respective parties took place in ensuing months but I do not recall any second meeting of the full Committee. The property interests of the University and the city seemed irreconcilable, as did apportionment of costs among all three parties. Many of these very clever people became highly sceptical of the whole enterprise on engineering and financial grounds; yet the concept of an inner ring road lingered for another four years, with the focus shifting towards the SW (Tollcross) quarter.

Edinburgh, St John's Road, Corstorphine

On the Glasgow road, successfully completed, a Woolworth's, supermarket & shops – but restricted to single storey because it was glebe land and the minister in the manse behind objected to the threatened view of the rear of an upper floor of one of the shops, although the only glimpse he could have got would have been out of his bathroom window by standing on his toilet seat.

Falkirk – High Street/ Bell's Wynd

Very successfully completed – a 2 phase scheme, closing Bell's Wynd and relocating the Bank of Scotland into the first phase before demolishing the large old Bank House which with its garden comprised the site for the second phase – the only snag being that the new premises were necessarily leasehold, which was heresy to the Bank, that had always owned freeholds. So I knew that a difficult meeting lay ahead for me with the great (later Sir) William Watson, General Manager (i.e. CEO) of the Bank no less, whose signature adorned its bank notes and who looked after "premises" in his spare time – nobody had heard of property departments or estate managers then. Sure enough, when he asked me with scornful distaste what would be the duration of this *lease* I realized that the normal 21 or even 42 years would not satisfy him so decided to go for broke and hastily suggested that, exceptionally, we could offer a lease as long as 99 years, whereupon he derisively hooted: *"99 years?"* It was like Lady Bracknell's *"A Handbag?"* He contemptuously added: "99 years in the life of the Bank of Scotland is (searching for the right word) *ephemeral*!" – with the result, as I recall, that we settled for something ridiculous like 250 years, three or four times the likely life of the building!

Glasgow, Hutchesontown/ Part Gorbals CDA

Successfully completed but a failure socially and commercially, having been won in a hyped competition promoted by the City to project a glossy and wholly artificial image for the "New Gorbals" by creating a shopping and leisure centre, with roof-top car-parking (in the Gorbals!) alongside Basil Spence's prize-winning tower blocks with the famous splayed pilotis (stilts) which, of course, were also demolished long ago. Politicians and local authorities today constantly talk about services for "the community" without defining either its composition or its extent: it is a buzz word for exploitation of power and public money – but it was in the promotion of this Glasgow district centre that I first heard that handy euphemism bandied about. There was no "district", since the area lacked any delineation or character, and a "centre" could not be created out of nothing in the middle of nowhere, on a site dominated by the adjoining cluster of tower blocks housing 400 flats – and just across the river from the bustling city centre. A feature in 'The Scotsman' on 22 June 1962 reported:

"The eight-acre site has been leased to the Murrayfield Company for 99 years at an annual rent of £17,275. The development scheme provides for 39 shops, two kiosks, two restaurants, a bank and some small service trade workshops. Parking facilities will also be provided for over 400 vehicles. *"While we hope this scheme is tailor-made for the location",* said Mr Linacre, *"the point is that here we have an opportunity for the development of a new, comprehensive shopping and cultural centre. We hope that this will prove to be a model of its kind."* In addition to the houses and shops, the development plan makes provision for three public houses, a National Assistance Office, and a medical block which might be used by two group practices as well as providing child welfare facilities. Space has also been reserved for a theatre, cinema and other recreational amenities. The city's planning convener (Councillor George Robertson) said he was completely satisfied."

'The Glasgow Herald' of the same date clarified that (after the first 18 months rent-free period to cover the building programme) the basic £17,275 annual ground rent would (a) be supplemented by one third of any excess over £85,000 in the actual net income received from the completed development and (b) itself be subject to uplift in line with periodic sub-lease rent reviews: perhaps the first instance of this formula which soon became commonplace.

The public houses and National Assistance Office (which effectively traded off each other) survived rather longer than the rest. But at the time everybody, including me, mistook all this wishful thinking for reality. So much local authority planning and procurement is at best ignorant idealism or, at worst, mere self-promotion. It is even worse today, since 'vibrant', 'dynamic', 'commitment' and 'delivery' have come to dominate the official vocabulary.

Glasgow, 1088-1092 Pollockshaws Road / Elephant Cinema / 62-70 Kilmarnock Road

An ambitious open-sided shopping precinct with roof-top car-parking, prominently sited at Shawlands, the fork of two major roads south of the city centre, designed by an English architect Maurice Day who had persuaded Walter Flack to take it on a year before I arrived. It was bedevilled by detailed design, construction and retail management difficulties from the start. Eventually it was completed and a civic opening ceremony organized; a shop unit equipped as a hospitality suite and, on the Kilmarnock Road frontage a red ribbon for the Lord Provost to cut. This was in winter, but the City Chambers belatedly advised that our guests might not arrive before 3.00pm, instead of 12.00 noon as originally requested, so there was no time to arrange for flood-lighting. Sure enough, word came through that the civic party was delayed at an official lunch, while the crowd waited – and further delayed – until long after 4.00, by which time the crowd had dispersed and the street-lights were on.

Eventually we saw the flashing blue lamp of a police outrider followed by headlights of the LP's limo, which pulled up in front of the red tape. The rear door was opened for our principal guest to get out, which he did with great difficulty. He staggered up a couple of steps onto the pavement, the ceremonial scissors placed carefully in his hand which was then guided towards the tape. This feat performed, he delivered his speech, which consisted of an announcement to the effect that "I need a drink", so he was escorted directly to the VIP suite, improvised from one of the shell units, where he remained until persuaded to return to George Square, by which time it was pitch dark. Maurice Day and the other professionals and the rest of us, including particularly Alan Wright who had come up from London for the occasion, scarcely met him, while the carefully rehearsed tour of the development was forgotten. That did not prevent us from putting out a press release trumpeting the event, nor from writing to thank the LP for making it such a success, to which his office replied to say how much he had enjoyed it and how impressed he was with the whole project.

Greenock, town centre redevelopment

Won in competition before I arrived, but detailed design, planning procedures, negotiation of financial terms and drafting of legal documentation had all been taking too long. However, a long-standing engagement had still to be honoured; for in the flush of publicity attending Murrayfield's nomination, Greenock's world-renowned Burns Club (which counted most of the Burgh's civic heads among its members) had extended the immense honour to Walter Flack of an invitation to propose the toast to the Bard's Immortal Memory at its Burns Supper in January 63 – one of the most important dates in the town's social calendar. Walter, who had never heard of haggis and didn't know the difference between a Burns Supper and a Rotary Club dinner, had meanwhile forgotten about this commitment, until three weeks beforehand, after the Christmas and New Year holiday.

Being obliged to accompany him, I tried vehemently to impress upon him what a hallowed, august occasion lay ahead and how vital it was that he did his homework – that here was the golden opportunity for him to cement relations between the company and this proud Burgh – but even driving out from Glasgow I still could not get him to take it seriously: Walter Flack was never awe-struck by anybody or anything. With no time to spare, he nevertheless insisted on spending half an hour wandering round the site of our project before strolling nonchalantly across to the magnificent Victorian Town Hall, where our hosts were waiting impatiently. Escorted into the glittering chamber, laid out as for a state banquet with chandeliers blazing, Walter was suddenly confronted with the momentous, intimidating reality of the situation whereupon, turning to me, he hissed, "Vivian, you should have warned me."

Bewildered by the ritual that followed, he duly found himself on his feet to perform the star role but, as in a waking nightmare, he could only tell a series of appalling Jewish jokes under the spontaneously improvised guise of the "Rabbi Burns", to which the audience listened in horrified silence. That disaster, from which Walter's infinitely resilient temperament quickly recovered, was never mentioned again, but dealings with the Council collapsed and the project was abandoned – I forget whether geological or title difficulties were blamed – until revived by a young developer some fifteen years later in a modified form, after the market recovered from the 74-77 crash.

Inverness, Bridge Street

Shops on the continuation of the High Street, below the Castle, descending to the crossing of the River Ness, with a public library and restaurant on the podium deck above. Acquired just as I was joining the company, without my involvement.

Lanark, 111-119 High Street 108-116 North Vennel

Successfully completed, supermarket and shop units, like Bathgate and Bearsden. This was a standard and highly profitable package, although before expiry of the initial occupational lease the supermarket unit had invariably become far too small and had to be divided to create two or three shop units or relet, e.g. to a cheap discount store or frozen food store.

Londonderry, 24-26 Ferryquay St/ Linenhall Street

This was an aberration, prompted by a friend of Walter's who was MD of Alfred Macalpine's (related to Sir Robert's) in Northern Ireland and wondered what could we do with this prominent corner site. It was very rough road from Belfast, after crossing with the car from Stranraer, to what was then the very isolated and alien city of Londonderry. An even greater shock was to discover the extent of political oppression of the Catholic minority (my Macalpine hosts were brazen about it) and to feel the threat of imminent civic unrest. But we went ahead, reassured by two options: ideally to create two large, three-storey units, one adjacent to F W Woolworth's and the other on the corner, failing which to provide an extension to Woolworth's store which was obviously too small. 'The Belfast Telegraph' of 7 May 1963 reported:

"The Murrayfield Real Estate Company – a subsidiary of the City Centre Group which is controlled by Mr Jack Cotton and Mr Charles Clore – may embark on extensive development in Northern Ireland if the pilot scheme, now being undertaken in Londonderry, proves a success.... The premises acquired by the developers were formerly owned by Irvine & Co. (Derry) Ltd., the city's oldest retail drapery store. Next door to Woolworth's in Ferryquay Street, the site extends along Upper Linenhall Street as far as the ABC cinema car-park. It is adjacent to the Richmond Street-Linenhall Street area, which Derry Corporation has earmarked for redevelopment as a modern shopping and business centre."

But there were no obvious tenants to pay adequate rents for these outsize units, guesstimates of development costs fluctuated alarmingly, it was too remote from Glasgow to administer efficiently, and fear of political violence was rising – which was stupid, because at worst we would have made a fortune out of government compensation courtesy of the UK taxpayer – so we settled for a soft option of ground-leasing the whole site to Woolies as a long-term investment. What happened subsequently – what form of development materialized – I never heard.

Motherwell – proposed Brandon Street CDA

Initiated during my regime but implemented after my departure. I had struggled to make progress, but later, under the personal direction of Alan Wright it became, with its subsequent phases, a hugely successful and profitable shopping and civic centre development. My main obstacle was the factor of the Duke of Hamilton's Estates, the 'Superior Landlords', from whom the 'heritable proprietors' held their titles, which were virtually freehold but subject to absurdly archaic restrictions, mainly dating from the 18thC when the area was largely agricultural, contained in their 'feu charters' (as explained earlier) that nobody had taken literally for generations but which he saw the opportunity of exploiting by seeking to charge huge 'grassums' (premiums) as payment for 'minutes of waiver', quoting sums which would have represented most of the notional uplift in value following relief. I foolishly allowed myself to get bogged down in this issue, because the legal mechanics and valuation implications interested me academically, even meeting him with the Duchess in the Duke's absence at her home in Eaton Square to try, in vain, to hammer out a viable formula; but of course all this mediaeval racketeering was subsequently stamped out by the feudal reform legislation.

Musselburgh – 132-134 High Street

Successfully completed – a tiny development of shops.

Stirling – 72-74 Murray Place

Successfully completed – an atrocity in concrete, a style had had become prevalent throughout the 60's – containing a couple of shop units in a prime pitch, undertaken solely in order to brighten the balance-sheet.

Some twenty projects, of which several were in hand prior to my arrival and several others never materialized and the rest initiated and completed, all within a period of 33 months. This bonanza was possible only because the market was still so naive.

'Sensitivity analysis' had not yet been invented, but I was conscious, for every project within Murrayfield's control, that in each case it was necessary to identify the most critical factor, by calculating the effects on the outcome of variations plus-or-minus in each factor, the most critical being that producing the most disproportionate variations and consequently the relatively greatest effect on the outcome.

Although no more than an improvised exercise, this often yielded startling results, because of the gross imbalance in most cases among the various principal factors, which in crude terms normally comprised: cost of site including legals, estimated development cost including design team fees, short and long-term rates of interest on borrowed capital, rental income forecast, projected investment yield and estimate duration (cost of time on interest charges and delayed income), letting fees and advertising. Though now greatly refined, that technique has not changed.

In 1963 I won 1st Prize in the Junior Members (under 35, which I was just) essay competition of the Incorporated Society of Valuers & Auctioneers, of which I was that year elected a Fellow – as mentioned earlier, it was later absorbed into the Royal Institution of Chartered Surveyors – a competition I had entered because the subject was "The Requirements of Good Development", about which by that time I thought I knew everything. The award was presented at the 1964 Annual Conference held in Torquay where I stayed over-night before the return journey – a long way by train to collect a cheque for 30 guineas!

That I learnt and produced so much so quickly was not only due to the benign and susceptible state of the market and huge potential demand in face of weak competition but also to the excellent basic training acquired at Healey & Baker, as well as to the inspiration provided by Walter Flack who died, tragically, in March 63 – less than two months after that Greenock fiasco – at the shockingly early age of 47. I had known him for just two, tumultuous and phenomenally productive years.

Railway Sites Ltd.

One mad episode that I shared with Walter, typical of the era in its naive enthusiasm, was Railway Sites Ltd., a company set up by British Rail on the incredibly amateurish assumption that all it had to do was identify the railway stations, goods yards, etc., with obvious (re)development potential (i.e. most of them), then prepare particulars with a very sketchy planning brief, and offer them all to a consortium of well-known developers, who would, in theory, compete fiercely among themselves for each and every project but in practice, predictably, proceeded to allocate the respective sites according to individual companies' special interests. Walter and I took part in the meeting of the consortium convened to deal with properties in Scotland, but held, of course, in London for the benefit of the big boys, some of whom had hardly ever crossed the Border.

Minutes apparently were not kept, and the entire proceedings were so fantastic that I have little recollection of the *dramatis personae* except for the dominance exerted by the mighty Joe Levy of D E & J Levy (who never practised in Scotland but upon whose skills and connections many English developers heavily relied) and his occasional partner Robert Clark, originally a Paisley solicitor turned developer who master-minded the epoch-making Euston Centre. It was just like a game of Monopoly, but with no money changing hands – simply horse-trading. ".......I'll swop you Glasgow Central, and as its leasehold I'll throw in Helensburgh, in exchange for Aberdeen Goods...."

Gifting the consortium a monopoly, free from obligation or commitment, and leaving its members to divide the spoils privately among themselves, effectively deprived Railway Sites of any prospect of securing a fair deal anywhere. The twin theory of this misbegotten strategy was that it would ensure a comprehensive programme producing massive results quickly; but that proved equally counter-productive. Having secured exclusive rights to whatever sites they wanted, the various developers had no incentive to hurry; and in every case, naturally, difficulties soon emerged relating to title or access or ground conditions or planning permission or the usual commercial risks. Bill Nethery, in sole charge of Railway Sites Ltd in Scotland, a very nice man but hopelessly out of his depth, died suddenly. I'm not sure that even one solitary project ever actually materialized. The British Railways Board soon set up a separate, high-powered organization to rationalize and oversee development of BR's vast estate.

But even today, nearly fifty years later, many local authorities are dealing with redevelopment or conservation or regeneration of their town centres or rural areas in just as foolhardy a fashion. Who is there, after all, to teach them? Consultant surveyors, commonly engaged to provide Councils with "independent, expert advice", can generally undertake excellent research in order to specify precisely what is wanted but rarely possess adequate practical experience of the relevant genre (shopping centre, office complex or whatever) to avoid the risk of stifling originality in competing developers' proposals, so tend to play safe by opting for the conventional that would be out of date by the time it is completed. Particularly in shopping development, an inside knowledge of trends is vital: if a concept is not original to the extent of projecting future trends it is already out of date!

Most planning authorities are too small to handle such enterprises and consequently too vulnerable to political pressures and business interests. To do their job efficiently, in protecting and promoting their environment, heritage, physical and financial assets, they need wider areas of competency. But the fundamental problem is that officers cannot perform professionally because they have to take instructions from committees of local politicians. We need a broader bottom tier, with essential parochial powers – unpaid members serviced by only a clerk and a treasurer – below large local authorities serviced by much smaller numbers of highly paid councillors, effectively commissioners, competent to supervise the officers without forever getting in their way.

I digress again! As I was saying, Walter Flack commanded rare loyalty and admiration for his sheer dynamism and bravado, his disregard for the rules, his love of company and, most of all, of ***his*** company. From humble beginnings – I don't know, but presume his (grand)parents were refugees from Central Europe – he qualified as a surveyor, I believe with Marcus Leaver, in 1938, just in time to join the army at the outbreak of war, where he rose to the rank of sergeant in the 8th Army in North Africa under General (later Field Marshal Sir) Claude Auchinleck, facts of which he was intensely proud, to such an extent that when he acquired the perfect vehicle, a ready-made, dormant Scottish public company (registered 1895 and with "real estate" in its title), he invited "the Auk" to become Chairman.

Incidentally, the term 'real estate' originated here, was exported to North America in the 17thC with Scots emigrants and reimported from the USA in the 19th. The Murrayfield Real Estate Co. Ltd. was formed to feu plots (again, Scots and Americans prefer "lots") for house-building in the wealthy Edinburgh suburb of that name. The City of Aberdeen Land Association, incorporated in 1875 – the first Scottish company to be listed on the London Stock Exchange – had similar origins and has since become CALA, the upmarket house-builder.

Walter's hero was the great Victorian engineer, Isambard Kingdom Brunel, whose name he bestowed on his yacht, which was built at Felixstowe. The launch must have been one of the happiest days of his life. As a good surveyor, all loved saying she was "72 feet overall and cost "72,000 – a thousand pounds a foot – that's fair, isn't it?" Though that, I suspect, was the price for only the hull. Whether he ever sailed in her I never heard; so far as I recall she was permanently moored on the Thames in Westminster, used for entertaining guests and show-girls from Murray's Cabaret Club.

He was a *bon viveur* and loved high society. In his office he employed as his PRO the property correspondent of *The Evening Standard*, Montgomery

Sharp, and also for a year or two, as what today would be called an intern, young Dickon Lumley, the future Earl of Scarbrough.

Turner

Stories are legendary concerning his volatile relationship with Turner, his chauffeur. Walter was always running late, and if on the way to an important meeting he would keep up an abusive commentary from the back of the Rolls, blaming Turner's driving for the delay: "You're in the wrong lane again.....you've let that taxi carve you up.....go on – the lights are changing", and so forth, which Turner knew was just the boss's way of pumping up the adrenalin in readiness for battle. But once, when they were stuck in a jam on the crown of the carriageway in the middle of Parliament Square, only a few hundred yards from their destination, Walter went too far, firing insults that Turner couldn't take, so he snapped "Then drive the ****ing thing yourself!", pulled on the handbrake, switched off the engine and stormed off.

But by the time he got home to Fulham he had calmed down and was feeling remorseful, a mood intensified by his wife's response: "You know what Walter's like, he was just working himself up as usual – now you've thrown away a lovely job – you'd better go into Neale House first thing tomorrow to return your uniform and things and hope that he gives you a good reference!" *[This is an imaginative reconstruction but according to Turner himself, later, accurate enough]* So in he went, very early, but the office junior was already there, and immediately called out, "Turner, thank God you're here: the governor's looking for you", so Turner, in a daze, pulled himself together and ran upstairs to the inner sanctum, whereupon Walter, with a wicked gleam in his eye, bellowed: "Turner, late as usual, have you forgotten where we're going?" To which the poor chap, utterly bewildered, could only stammer: "Er, no, of course not, Walter, but....but where's the car?" Whereupon Walter, with triumphant glee, hurled the keys across the room, yelling: "Where you ****ing left it!" For when Turner had stormed off, Walter had simply reached forward, taken the keys out of the ignition, locked the car and walked to the venue for his appointment, confident that the Rolls could be safely left overnight in one of the busiest spots in London, and so it proved – fifty years ago there were no traffic wardens and only a fraction of today's volume of traffic. Chutzpah!

Walter died in his bath in Whitehall Court, that vast, ostentatious Victorian pile occupying a whole block down Northumberland Avenue facing the Embankment, which not only witnessed his demise but had also, ironically, caused the downfall of his beloved company the previous year. I happened to be in London in 1962 during his tense negotiations to acquire it – a complex of venerable clubs and apartments that would obviously be a management nightmare but offered enormous potential – when on impulse he suggested we took the car for a drive around it, as if going to have yet another look might ease the stress of arriving at a decision on his final bid. So we cruised around that block very slowly while, as in a trance, he stared fixedly through the windows that remained closed, as he muttered something like "It's got to be worth a million quid, hasn't it?" He was not expecting a response nor would have heard any, for he was only trying to convince himself.

Whatever the actual figure, he succeeded, but then discovered (so Goble, Trueblood and I gathered) that he didn't have the cash for settlement. So he had to take desperate action, which was to go cap in hand to the mighty Jack Cotton in his suite at the Dorchester Hotel. This humiliating experience proved effective, but the upshot was that control of Murrayfield passed to Cotton's huge property company.

Jack Cotton

How Walter could have exchanged contracts, committing the company to such a major acquisition, without having the funds available, I never knew and cannot imagine, but Walter was left utterly demoralised. My next visit to London was to attend a board meeting held in one of the magnificent drawing-rooms in Whitehall Court, with "the Auk" in the chair, looking bewildered, the florid Jack Cotton in one of his loud suits and bow-tie, like a wealthy book-maker, totally dominating proceedings, and a very subdued Walter Flack, of whom my last memory was in Neale House, a few months before he died, looking miserable. All I could think of saying then was that he would always be my Uncle Walter, which raised half a smile.

Jack Cotton was an extrovert Birmingham estate agent turned developer, chiefly famous for a massive office development in New York – the Panam Building – which was even the subject of an advertising lyric, "The biggest office building in the world". Although not nearly a skyscraper its bulk was indeed colossal. Cotton merged his company with Charles Clore's to create the no. 1 property development company of the age, City Centre Properties, that embraced its own building company, Token Construction, briefly notorious for building the Hilton Hotel on Park Lane, whose top floors threatened the privacy of Kensington and Buckingham Palaces' gardens. For a while, even in Scotland, we were expected to negotiate all building contracts with Token, which caused one or two near-disasters until that policy was restricted to London – or maybe Token was disposed of.

Walter's death devastated Alan Wright (two years my junior, as were both Trueblood and Goble), who had been Walter's boy from the beginning. But he bore up heroically, defending the company's interests with amazing maturity in face of huge pressures from City Centre. He regained virtual autonomy when the group was sold to Land Securities Investment Trust (the new no.1), whose two development subsidiaries were given equal billing, Murrayfield in Scotland and Ravenseft in England (inevitably merged later), which was ironic, considering that only four years earlier Ravenseft had been my client at H&B as the originally nominated developer for Dundee Overgate until ousted by Murrayfield! But meanwhile, under Alan Wright, Murrayfield had forged ahead with its own development programme in the Midlands and Scotland with tremendous success.

Cotton had died, too, just a year after Flack, having been overpowered by Clore, just as Flack had been overpowered by Cotton. But Clore was not just a property man; he was running a conglomerate, so left Alan Wright very much alone to run his own show.

Frank Price also grieved for his great friend but settled into partnership with his successor, exerting an ever-widening influence from his powerhouse in Birmingham, the city of which he remained a Councillor until 1975, becoming Lord Mayor 64-65 and thereafter Deputy Lieutenant, not only of Warwickshire 70-82, but also of West Midlands 74-82 and of Herefordshire & Worcestershire 73-82 (an unprecedented full set!), as well as Chairman of both Telford New Town Corporation 68-72 and, thanks to his friendship with (Lord) Richard Marsh, the British Waterways Board 68-74.

A piece in *Private Eye* entitled "How Labour looks after its own" reported that the explanations by the respective spokesmen were that the Chairman's remuneration was low because it was a part-time appointment and that it was high because it was a full-time appointment. But Frank's great love was children's musical education, founding and chairing the Midlands Art Centre for Young People '60-66, for which, specifically, he was knighted in 1966. To cap it all, he was appointed Chairman of National Exhibition Centre Ltd. 70-76, an Honorary Fellow of the Royal Institution of Chartered Surveyors and a Freeman of the City of London. Not bad for a tool-maker to trade!

But Alan Wright was now running a very tight ship, with the emphasis quite rightly on management and on his own pet projects, which in Scotland meant mainly Dundee, Motherwell and Glenrothes (a recently won project), which did not need me. The bold buccaneering days were over. I was merely one of Clore's many minions and far removed from the decision-making process. The Board of the Scottish subsidiary, of which I was nominally M.D., never met. No doubt a secretary in Neale House composed the Minutes of its AGM and filed them away. Time, once again, to move on. Alan Wright wanted to renew my contract but made no attempt to dissuade me when I declined.

It may well have been very short-sighted to quit Healey & Baker, but it was right to quit Murrayfield, which was no longer a creative environment. Besides, other major development companies, already active in Scotland, wanted to set up shop there, and by now all the premier league firms of commercial property surveyors from London had opened or were about to open a Scottish office and even a few indigenous practices had sprung up as the market was maturing fast.

But I could not walk out of Murrayfield and straight into a rival company; I promised Alan Wright I would not even think of that. So I needed a one-man band to employ me for a year at most, to serve as 'quarantine'. That man was Walter Harris JP, a Glasgow entrepreneur with nice offices in Park Circus who fancied becoming another Izzy Walton. By the mid-60s there was a rash of these mini or micro-mini- tycoons in every major city who knew nothing about commercial property but had made (or had access to) the odd hundred thousand pounds and assumed that all that was required was to hire a qualified chap from one of the big agents, pay him a year's salary and you'd make a bundle.

Walter Harris and his brother Ernest had built up a small chain of shops in prime locations combining, in front, the sale of premium brands of pipe tobacco, cigarettes and cigars, and, through in the back, a gentlemen's hairdressing salon. But the brothers had apparently fallen out and Ernest continued the business, leaving Walter with little to do apart from running a 'tartan tat' wholesale supply company operating out of Renfrew Airport. But he was happy enough, with a son at Gordonstoun in the same House as Prince Charles (but then, wasn't everybody's son who attended that School in the same House as HRH, just as everybody of the appropriate age who attended Fettes was Tony Blair's fagmaster?) and a plaque on his desk announcing that he was a 'Name' at Lloyd's.

He had imposing letterheads printed for an investment company as our new vehicle as well as for 'Thornton Linacre Associates' to be our fee-earning professional front; but my private resolve that this would be a short engagement was reinforced when, for no apparent purpose other than to impress me and my wife, he invited us to dinner in the North British Hotel in

Edinburgh (now the Balmoral) but first insisted that we were escorted on an imperious tour of the (very busy) kitchens, at the end of which he tipped the Head Chef half a crown; an embarrassment which deprived me of any appetite. I bought half a dozen shops in good suburban locations around Glasgow and let them to show a net return well in excess of the cost of servicing his capital, but I was only marking time until – sure enough – the right invitation arrived.

From friendly architects and surveyors, I learnt that they were working on one or two interesting projects undertaken by the London-based City Wall Properties Ltd., which had recently gone public. Then on one of his Scottish site visits I was invited to meet their development director, Edward James, with whom I got on famously right away.

He in turn invited me to London to meet his Chairman, Henry Oppenheim, joint managing directors, Arthur Berg and Derek Montague, and staff architect Ernest Petter. I was greatly encouraged in this by my old buddy Roderick Maclean, whom I had succeeded in charge of Scotland at Healey & Baker and then again at Murrayfield and who – having been effectively made redundant by Alan Wright whose own professional agency, Walter Flack Wright & Partners had replaced Walter Flack Maclean & Wright to take direct control – had now secured commissions from this major newcomer, City Wall Properties, a company unfamiliar with Scotland.

7 AMBITION

According to legend, City Wall Properties quit their original offices in City Wall House in the City because the basement car-park was accessed from a lane at the back by way of a spiral ramp, on which the bends were too tight for the Chairman's long-nosed Italian sports-car to negotiate; but I prefer to believe that it resulted from a brilliant redevelopment by his team of a whole block on Brompton Road (nos. 163-169), in which the entire ground and first floors were let to Austin Reed, who had long wanted a Knightsbridge store, while the top floor was designed for opulent penthouses, leaving the two middle floors to let as offices, of which the directors decided that one would provide ideal new company headquarters.

City Wall were very good at offices, having built three blocks in Croydon, each named after one of Henry & Sally Oppenheim's children – Philip House, Rosanne House and another. Retail was not their forte; yet, ironically, perhaps their most spectacular coup in my time was in consequence of the acquisition of a large site in Northampton with a view to promoting an ambitious retail warehouse park, a project which failed for reasons which I have forgotten, with the result that they had no option but to fall back on offices, half-heartedly planning a business park, which they promptly, by accidentally miraculous timing, pre-let in its entirety to Barclays Bank as the HQ for its brand-new Barclaycard – Britain's pioneering credit card: a stupendous outcome.

Edward James was my immediate boss – the best I ever had – we got on perfectly for six years. His elder sister was Phyllis, P D James the novelist, later Baroness James of Holland Park. But until I joined the main board in 1971, I did not know Henry Oppenheim well. Nobody meeting such a suave metropolitan would guess that he was born in Glasgow – his explanation was that "I decided when three years of age to go to London to make my fortune" – but one cousin, the very Glaswegian Myer Oppenheim became a major furniture retailer trading as James Grant and also founded the very successful property development company Argyll Securities, although Henry never spoke of him. Nor did he speak of Myer's brother Harold, who became an eminent Edinburgh City Councillor: the brothers had owned James Grant jointly but they split the business giving Myer the major James Grant (West) and leaving Harold with the minor James Grant East, but later he too concentrated on property.

I was warned that, despite a charming, quiet exterior, Henry could explode with rage in face of incompetency. Perhaps the best illustration – each time I heard the story it was slightly embellished and my affectionate retelling will no doubt embroider it even more – concerned the momentous occasion on which, in the magnificent, newly completed mansion, modestly named 'Barons Court', which he and Sally had designed and built on Winnington Road next to The Bishops Avenue, the fabulous "Millionaire's Row" in Hampstead, he welcomed a party of business associates as his first guests. This is purely anecdotal as I was not present, but it seems he proudly ushered them from the portico into the double-height entrance hall and there demonstrated the spectacular lighting controls, the huge chandelier flanked on either side by twin elliptical staircases which they ascended to a gallery facing double doors. Flinging them open for his guests to enter the grand drawing room, he stood back in order to switch off the entrance hall lights and blazing chandelier before stepping inside to join them. But he then discovered to his horrified disbelief that there were no lighting controls on the gallery. Silently seething, while outwardly the smiling, gracious host, he served drinks and conversed until, at the first opportunity, he slipped out, raced down the stairs, switched off the theatrical lights and ran back up the dimmed staircase, while bearing mind throughout the rest of the evening that towards the end he would need another chance to withdraw in order to run down again in the dark and switch them back on. Having done that and having seen his guests off around midnight, he got busy on the telephone.

He called the architect's home number and got him out of bed, summoning him to an urgent site meeting but refusing to disclose the nature of the disaster until he arrived: likewise the quantity surveyor, the structural and services engineers, the main contractor, site agent and electrical contractor. (Telephone enquiries then were efficient and free!) Once they had arrived, mostly by taxi, several from across London, looking dishevelled and bemused, seeing no sign of a catastrophe, the first of them to get there having to hang about for nearly an hour until the last one turned up, their client then addressed the assembled, bemused and by now extremely anxious company. He quietly thanked them all for coming, apologized for interrupting their sleep, and invited them to admire the lighting controls in the entrance hall before ushering them up the stairs to the gallery. There he once more flung open the doors into the grand salon, but this time entered first, turning around to invite the others to follow while calling upon them as they came in to switch off the downstairs lights.

Muttered confusion broke, then consternation. Henry told them to hurry up, asking if anything was wrong, whereupon some poor soul had to reveal that there did not appear to be any lighting control on the gallery. Thereupon their client launched into his mentally rehearsed and memorized tirade: "Every semi-detached on a spec. builder's estate – every one-up-and-two-down council house – has a two-way switch at the top of the stairs.......we have the Blackpool Illuminations downstairs and not a glimmer above....you bunch of incompetents aren't fit to design a doghouse.....you should all be struck off and cast into the outer darkness......." and so forth until exhaustion set in; then dismissed them without a 'good night' or even a 'good bye'. Naturally, as so many well-known figures were present, it all got out and quickly circulated. Today it would be instantly tweeted and posted on Facebook. .

But at that time it could spread only by word of mouth, giving rise to wholesale improvisations and apocrypha, so becoming the stuff of legend and alive still today. To embody it in this brief history may seem uncharitable but, like the stories about Walter Flack, it is really a fond tribute to one of the original giants of the commercial property industry. Only a huge personality was capable of spontaneously devising and conducting such an exercise. There are no such heroes today.

Easterhouse

The most important development to which City Wall was already committed in Scotland was the Easterhouse Township Centre, won in competition promoted by Glasgow Corporation to provide a centre for one of the largest municipal housing estates in Europe, completely isolated on the Eastern outskirts of the city, developed in phases over many years yet without any central shopping or leisure facilities – another triumph of socialist planning! Having at last designated the location and nominated the developer, this Utopian authority then discovered that they would have to start again elsewhere, because the National Coal Board had suddenly revealed that the site in question was sitting above a large, rich seam of high-grade, brown coking coal which had yet to be extracted.

This necessitated relocation and replanning of the project and associated facilities, public transport, etc., at great expense and amid ludicrous mutual recriminations between the NCB and Council officers. I arrived in time to organize the marketing, lettings and management, with great support from the constituency MP, Hugh Brown, who acted as mediator with the Council when necessary, becoming a great friend and later a Junior Scottish Office Minister.

'The Scottish Daily Express" reported on 17 September 1968 – beneath the headline "The Shopping Bag Hecklers": "Four hundred and fifty angry tenants went to a protest meeting last night. They demanded action on plans to build a £3 million shopping centre at Easterhouse, Glasgow. The protesters – mostly women – were told that work was due to start *six years ago*. But delays had put the date back again and again. Then they threatened that unless suitable proposals were put forward at the meeting, in St. Leonard's School, they would seal off the whole Easterhouse scheme from Glasgow Corporation workmen as a protest. But after hearing a pledge that work would be under way by April, members of the Provanhill Tenants Association who organized the meeting agreed to call off their militant action. Their stormy meeting (police kept watch outside the school) was attended by the Provan Ward's MP Mr Hugh Brown. Also there were two of the ward's councillors, Mr Tom Fulton and Mrs Agnes Ballantyne, and Mr V Linacre, a senior director of City Wall Properties. They had to face a barrage of heckling and angry questions from the irate tenants. Mr Tom Fulton gave the reasons for the delay. "The Corporation had to negotiate with the Coal Board as there was a lot of coal underground in the area. Then an inquiry had to be held into the proposal to build a separate shopping centre just half a mile away."

That interloping scheme was known as Garrowhill (i.e. Baillieston) with a huge frontage to the South side of the main Edinburgh Road. I had to prepare the formal objection to the inquiry on behalf of City Wall, in which I was accidentally helped by a hapless assistant employed by the architect for the rival developers who had to transport the scale model of their scheme hurriedly from London for display in Glasgow, discovering to his horror on arrival that one of what were meant to represent twin blocks of offices had come adrift, but he – in a panic and not being familiar with that element of the design – assumed that what was meant to represent a very tall block had broken in two and so got hold of some glue and carefully stuck the loose part back on top, with the result that this tower was the main feature in the press photographs taken at the inquiry and attracted the strongest objections.

Easterhouse was Scotland's first enclosed shopping mall. We were exploring virgin territory. So among several innovations that I had to devise were formulae for allocation of service charges per unit, to reconcile rental values with floor area – they had to be equated because service charges clearly could not equitably be based solely on one or the other – in collaboration with the most erudite, cultured, colleague I ever knew, our Glasgow lawyer William L Taylor.

He served for six years as Convener (Chairman) of the city's Housing Committee, responsible for planning and implementing those aforesaid 29 Comprehensive Development Areas which comprised not only the massive slum clearance programme (the 'overspill' strategy mentioned earlier) but also the highly successful ring road, the route of which – by *real*, integrated planning – largely replaced that inner belt of slums that for a hundred years had wrapped around the city centre. The City Chambers joked that he built the Kingston Bridge as a short cut home to Pollokshields from his office at Charing Cross. But the only reward for his monumental service to the city was a belated CBE. He was due to be elected Lord Provost, but those Councillors who had gone away in the armed forces during the war never forgave him for having done his national service in a civilian capacity as a conscientious objector; so they elected the City's first Lady Lord Provost instead!

The Township Centre was immensely successful for thirty years, but then suddenly declined in face of improved public transport and growth in car-ownership and increasingly accessible retail parks, supermarkets and leisure facilities, until it was refurbished and transformed as the Shandwick Centre, and is now going down for the second time. The days of 'District Centres', comprising a cross-section of specialist retailers to serve a local catchment, are over.

That tier in the old hierarchy has been eliminated – it simply fell out of use. Everything it offered can be found in one mega-supermarket. Soon there will be traditional but much condensed town and city centres; a few regional centres, stand-alone mega-supermarkets and retail parks (often incorporating cinemas or bowling alleys); but nothing at all between all those large-scale organisms and local neighbourhood strips (parades). Easterhouse and so many centres of that scale served their purpose during that evolutionary period; they had the same life-span as tower blocks of council flats, most of which have recently been or are being blown up – many of them still with years ahead of continuing capital cost repayments.

Tollcross

Having monitored very closely the saga of Edinburgh's misbegotten ring road scheme, it still seemed, more than two years after the University side of it had been abandoned, as if the SW corner might yet proceed in some modified form, because (a) it could provide a direct link (inner relief road) to the A8 and Airport, (b) the whole Tollcross area did undoubtedly need a drastic overhaul of both traffic and buildings, and c) in the period immediately prior to development of the St James Centre there was a huge unsatisfiable demand for shopping floor-space in the city centre. So once again I found myself immersed in traffic planning with the same Corporation officials and several of the same councillors, but wearing a City Wall instead of a Murrayfield hat – and once again secured the nomination as prospective developers, though with a different design team – more of my own choosing. Much of the credit, admittedly, was due to the Standard Life Assurance Co. Ltd., in those days an independent giant insurance company, which had a large share-holding in City Wall and was its principal source of funding, sometimes on critically favourable terms as in this instance.

The front page of 'The Edinburgh Evening News' on 25 November 1966 carried the headline: "Shopping area Traffic free by 1970 -- £2 million Tollcross plan to set the pattern for Europe" above the story: "Tollcross, a giant traffic-free shopping centre for the 1970s. That's the image set today by the Scottish director of the development firm which will spend £2 million there. "Tollcross is going to be restored to its former pre-eminence, winning back shoppers it has lost to the West End", said Mr V Thornton Linacre, resident director of City Wall Properties (Scotland) Ltd. of Glasgow. The company have just been appointed developers for the Tollcross shopping centre, entailing 300,000 square feet of shopping space spread over a traffic-free precinct covering eight acres. Edinburgh Corporation will build the huge raised traffic roundabout which will skirt the shopping area. Passing over it from Melville Drive will be the city's new inner ring road. Mr Linacre said today: "This is one of the most enlightened schemes of the type in Europe as a solution to traffic-pedestrian problems." Mr Linacre said that research and other preliminary work would take 18 months to 2 years. This would be carried out while the statutory procedures required of the Corporation went on – Treasury approval for road projects, public inquiries and government consultation. Six developers negotiated with the Corporation for the Tollcross project. City Wall were officially named by the planning committee yesterday."

Over a year-and-a-half later, on 27 June 1968, the same 'Evening News' duly reported – beneath the headline, 'It's the £10m. dream that will be Tollcross of the future':

"It won't be long now before big changes start happening around Tollcross way. The major part of its development plan has the go-ahead. And the only major problem now remaining is the details of the big dual carriageway which dives below the eight acre circular shopping precinct. The underground road – part of the approved southern half of the ring road – is in line with the original plans laid down for the Tollcross scheme. The underpass idea was changed in favour of an overpass when it was found that Tollcross was threaded below ground with a maze of sewers and cables and pipes, making it preferable economically to have the road up rather than down. Now the Secretary of State has quashed that idea and the city's engineers have had to go back to their original, more expensive scheme. The bill for the roadworks within Tollcross itself is likely to work out at £1 million. But as one city official phrased it laconically: 'It is likely to cost another £1 million 'just to dig the darned hole'. For the last eighteen months a big development company, City Wall Properties (Scotland) Ltd, have been carrying out surveys in preparation for a shopping and social centre originally estimated around £2 million but now expected to be closer to £3 million. But according to Mr Linacre, the potentialities of the new Tollcross are enormous. He says that in the next decade or so, Tollcross and the new St James Square-Leith Street area will become the major shopping centres in Edinburgh, drawing the 'quantity' trade and leaving the 'quality' trade to the big prestige stores in Princes Street. But the planners are apprehensive about the outcome of the decisions affecting the new underground through road, particularly in relation to its offshoots....

Under the previous plans with the elevated roadway, the slip roads were less of a problem and passing traffic was more easily attracted to the new shopping centre. The position might not be so straightforward now, but a great deal depends on the way in which the city engineers evolve their ideas for submission to the Secretary of State. But without easy offshoots, the shopping potential could suffer. The change in the construction of the new through road has already caused considerable concern, not only to the city and the developers, but also to the existing shopkeepers in the area. Last week the organisation representing Tollcross independent traders called on the Corporation for information and assurances about the progress of the scheme, which has had little public attention in the last two years since major plans were first announced. Mr Linacre is also anxious for speedy decisions. If delays are too great, he says, Tollcross could become subject to 'planning blight'........."

And so it proved. Whether underground or overhead, the engineering cost estimates, plus costs of property acquisitions – plus an inevitable public enquiry – proved utterly prohibitive. Another triumph of municipal planning! All that work in partnership with the Corporation and the University on one side of the ring road scheme and two years later in partnership again with the Corporation on another side of it – done for no purpose! An array of 'Consultants' and professional advisers will no doubt have been engaged during the course of this protracted fiasco, and assuredly well paid for their abortive services; but the frustrated developer, who was officially appointed by the Corporation in the first place and who has performed fully in accordance with their agreement, is not even formally dismissed after the City has ruined it, far less thanked for services rendered – and least of all paid for them! How ironic is the general assumption that the forever-maligned and caricatured developer can always afford to act *pro bono public*!

Erskine House

The initial deal preceding one other major development had also been struck just before I joined City Wall: the acquisition of the Mary Erskine School for Girls, towards the west end of Queen Street in the heart of the capital, from the school's owner and governing body, the Merchant Company of Edinburgh (an immensely influential and well-endowed corporation of mediaeval foundation), following the school's decision to move out of the city centre, where its Victorian buildings were obsolete, inadequate, lacking in any recreational space and surrounded by commercial premises that had long replaced the Georgian town houses. At Easterhouse, City Wall achieved Scotland's first enclosed shopping mall, and now we were to produce the very first speculative office development of any size in the city centre of Edinburgh, which we named City Wall House. (The name was unpopular with the planners because the location was so distant from the line of Edinburgh's Flodden Wall, but it served our promotional purposes.)

There was a muted chorus of objections to our detailed planning application, largely on nostalgic grounds, but a few also from those who had forgotten that the school was only 55 years old (and was never more than half built because of the outbreak of the Great War) and that it had replaced a stretch of the early 19th century terrace. Perversely, the only serious complaint to our proposed development came from the Edinburgh establishment who kept asking, "But who are you building it for?" They simply could not grasp the concept of speculative development. That mentality is still encountered among Labour local authorities today.

The only objection architecturally arose because at that time the whole street elevation was still black from pollution but we had found a quarry with the last cache of the original Craigleith stone, with the result that our facade was a gleaming pale yellow, prompting a prominent body of building conservationists (who shall remain anonymous in order to avoid reopening an old sore) to complain that we had used a non-conforming cladding material.

The main contractor, Kyle Stewart, presented me with an inscribed silver trowel after I had "topped out" the building on 30th May 1968. Meanwhile, planning the internal partitioning of the floors and corresponding services for letting purposes was proving very complicated and so I was greatly relieved when Ivory & Syme, the city's leading investment brokers (they then had little competition), whose offices were round the corner at 1-3 Charlotte Square, came up with an offer to take a head lease of the whole building, whereupon they sub-let almost the entire space to a stable of their own clients – and changed the name to Erskine House. Everybody happy – a quite superb project!

New Club

Yet another pioneering project was City Wall's redevelopment of the New Club on Prince's Street in Edinburgh, which again we won in a competition promoted by Hillier Parker on behalf of the Club. It embodied what was in effect the first-ever speculative retail scheme in the city centre. But it was much more ambitious than that, because the brief issued by the Club's agents (Hillier Parker) required City Wall as the developer to replace the great Victorian building with retail units on ground and first floors while allowing for a new street entrance and hallway leading to stairs and a lift connecting with a modern New Club occupying the whole of the upper floors. So the development profit represented the capital value of the excess rental income from the four shop-lettings after servicing the total capital cost. In effect the Club acquired magnificent, purpose-built new premises to their precise specification, with interiors which preserved its hallowed traditions yet incorporated all the latest technology and equipment, all at no cost except for a double removal: first into a small hotel just off St Andrew Square which they leased for three years, providing enough space and facilities to keep the Club functioning throughout the development programme – while everything not required meanwhile, and all their valuable possessions, were put into store elsewhere – following which the move back into their new home. This was a very exciting competition to win – it helped that the general manager of

Standard Life (Francis Jamieson), a main board director of City Wall, was a senior member of the Club.

But the capital city's entire elite were members of the Club! Indeed, when drafting the Head Agreement, we realized on both sides that the necessary Arbitration Clause, with provision for ultimate legal recourse, would be unenforceable since no High Court judge could take the case as everyone was a Club member; and consequently we had to substitute what (off the record) we called a "loving kindness clause" which essentially bound the parties on no account to engage in any dispute – and also to treat this improvisation as strictly confidential!

Forty years on, the building, inside and out, still looks in pristine condition, such was the exceptional quality of workmanship, particularly the granite elevational cladding and the beautiful dining-room, which is an exact replica of the original to the nearest mm, all the panelling, skirtings, dado and picture rails, doors, architraves and window surrounds being meticulously taken down by expert craftsmen, stored for the duration and restored where necessary, and at last triumphantly put back as if nothing had changed at all – an amazing feat of joinery genius!

My contribution was largely confined to letting the shops, making maximum use of the 1st floors which, of course, commanded wonderful views across Prince's Street Gardens to the Castle. The contractors and site agents taught me a lot and I also learnt a great deal by having to work for the first time alongside an Edinburgh establishment design team – architects, QS and engineers – most of whom suffered an even greater culture shock by having to work for the first time in their lives alongside a dastardly commercial developer! That prejudice lasted through the '74-'77 slump but the current one has put paid to it. When the first Chairman was appointed for the newly established Scottish Development Agency (c.1978), with a huge budget for public investment, I happened to be lunching in Edinburgh and there in the same restaurant was the whole High Society team – a tableau like The Last Supper – wining him and no doubt warning him against having anything to do with *hoi polloi.*

One early bonus during demolition of the old Club was to discover that the 6 feet-high urinal stalls in the vast lavatory were lined with thick, high-quality lead, the salvage value of which considerably reduced the price for the job. Before the Club finally committed themselves to the project there had been a number of diehard backwoodsmen who still refused to see the need for change but who relented when I took them on a tour of the 19th century 'domestic offices' – kitchens and staff quarters – which of course they had never seen before and from which they emerged subdued and abashed.

Trinity Park

Our fourth 'First' was Trinity Park, over a mile N of the city centre, Scotland's first major out-of-town office development. The idea arose from my first encounter with a strikingly talented new pair of architects, Jim Marshall and Mike Morison, who had quit the mighty firm of Robert Matthew Johnson-Marshall & Partners to set up on their own, on the strength of winning a competition for the design of Scotland's first electronics manufacturing plant, Hewlett Packard at South Queensferry. They told me that the Currie Shipping Line, part of the country's maritime history, with interests on the Clyde and in Leith, was preparing to sell its historic headquarters which, incongruously, was an old mansion house [which architecturally had no special merit] in acres of garden on the Ferry Road, the old highway connecting South Queensferry and Leith. It suddenly occurred to me/us that it could provide an ideal site for an office campus, the like of which nobody in the country had never seen, but which I was sure would work well because of the germinating demand for grade 'A' accommodation with large floor-plates, available here in a building with no need to go higher than three floors – so easy vertical and horizontal circulation – in addition to the obvious advantages of lavish car-parking, landscaping, high amenity, lots of local good-class labour, and easy access into the city as well as E & W. The planning authorities would support us (easing congestion downtown) but we had to overcome the automatic, instinctive objections by Edinburgh's conservation bodies and amenity societies. After the development was completed, the monthly magazine, 'SCOTLAND', published the story in its September 1972 issue:

"When your upper management man comes to live in Edinburgh, his house-hunting trail is not hard to follow: Ravelston, Barnton, Cramond, Morningside, Grange. And Trinity, where the heavy £20,000 stuff stands in big gardens and gazes down the slope to their owners' yachts in Granton Harbour. So it is easy to imagine the tide of outrage which rolled through Trinity one day in 1968, when the residents awoke to find that a seven-acre sylvan gem in their midst had been ear-marked for development; shops, offices, car-parks, the lot. Almost incredible, however, is how it all ended. What could have been another acrimonious punch-up evolved into a classic model of how urban development can proceed to the benefit of a city, commerce and the owners adjoining, with goodwill and confidence abounding.

"The story of the Trinity Cottage Affair is worth telling in some detail, for here, one of Britain's biggest developers, City Wall, displayed a technique so sophisticated yet so human, that their eventual planning application for a £1.5 million development went before the Committee, accompanied by written endorsement from the three bodies who had first sprung to arms.

"It all began when the management of the long-established Currie Line of ship-owners decided they must move from Trinity Cottage, their headquarters for many years, and take new offices for their amalgamation with Anchor Line. Their three-storeyed mansion was set behind a high stone wall in a seven-acre garden, studded with copper beeches, yews, ash, and the rarer growing things that had been returned by generations of deep-sea skippers. The site, on the edge of Trinity, yet only five minutes' drive from Princes Street, had enormous attractions for developers, and the bush telegraph was going before the Board decision to move had been written up. First in the field was Argyle Securities, the people who stitched together the project which saw slum tenements behind Edinburgh Castle replaced with a mighty government office block. Into this quiet, expensive backwater, Argyle proposed various mixed developments, including a shopping centre, office blocks, flats and multi-storey car-parks. The site was to be transformed beyond recognition. The local residents rose in wrath and effectively mustered forces. What followed was painful for Argyle and the Currie Line and the whole proposal was abandoned. When the Currie management had rubbed sufficient embrocation on the bruises, three other developers were quietly asked for their views on a future for Trinity Cottage and its grounds. All made the same point: because of the site value, the amenity lobby's wish for a pricy housing development was out of the question. It had to be a development for commerce.

"The man who impressed Currie was Vivian Linacre, City Wall's director in charge of Scottish developments. A neatly built, forceful, eloquent man, Linacre had other things going for him, like an Edinburgh education and upbringing, and experience as a surveyor in the city. He also had a hand that gentled Establishment people into letting City Wall tackle such star projects as the redevelopment of the Capital's New Club in Princes Street and Queen Street's Erskine House. Other projects with new towns, councils and companies had included Linwood Town Centre, the climatically controlled Easterhouse Township Centre, the big Glasgow complex at Shawlands Cross and the scheme that will bring some amenity and fun into the soulless tundra of Edinburgh's Wester Hailes housing development.

"Currie wanted to know what Linacre proposed to do about the opposition; the Trinity/Goldenacre Association, the Leith Civic Trust and the powerful Cockburn Association, all still manning the trenches. Linacre proposed that he should form a committee representing all of them in on the project from the start, with straight access to the architects, Marshall Morison Associates. As a first token of good faith, he would retain the high walls of mellow stone that enclosed the peninsular site and cheerfully submit to a Tree Preservation Order on the hundred-odd major trees within it. That package threw overboard most of the tenets of the developer. *[The editor actually missed a priceless howler by printing "threw overboard most of the tenants"]* He must usually initiate work in strictest secrecy and wants total flexibility on the site. Linacre seemed to have transmitted his position to the enemy, then sown his own arboreal minefield in which he could not move.

"His vindication can be seen today on the site of Trinity Cottage. Set incredibly in lush parkland, brushed by stately trees, ready to let, is 145,000sq.ft. of prime office space, capable of housing 1,200 [workers] with 350 cars. It is Scotland's first campus-style office development, a concept from the U.S. suburbs but unique in its proximity to a city's business centre. With service industries forming 74 percent of the Capital's employment and prime sites running out, it should bring prime rentals. Linacre and City Wall achieved this project by an impressive piece of mutual trust and kept promises.

"'We had to make sure that our scheme was acceptable to the amenity bodies from the start', he said. 'First, we charted the position of every tree of any size on the site. There were about 110. We met on site with the city planners, our architect and a tree surgeon and decided which of them were sick and which of them just had to come down to allow construction. In the end, not more than 10 percent of them were felled and all are being replaced.'

On 20 April 1970, about a dozen people, representing the amenity bodies met.....in Edinburgh and learned what City Wall had in mind. Literally, the building was shaped to fit in among the trees, looking at the end of the day "like a sick octopus", said Linacre. *[I was actually quoting one of the insults levelled at the plans by Derek Montague, Joint MD – another being 'like a melted swastika' – during my board room battle to gain formal approval, which was finally secured only by the Chairman's casting vote.]* But it had all the merits of the latest planning.....Best of all from the objectors' point of view, City Wall had listened to their arguments and had produced a major three-storey office block that was actually lower than the old Trinity Cottage. On their side, the objectors' representatives kept the promise of secrecy, restraining their people from external comment. When the time came in June to apply for planning permission in principle, all City Wall had to show the Council was a site plan and description of the development. Instead, the project was taken as far as design drawings, finishes, etc. In this way, the objectors' committee were convinced of how the project was going to look and cooperated in the gambit which met the wishes of a once-bitten careful Currie Line and assured its approval by the city. On 28th June 1970 the application for [outline] consent was lodged, in the name of the Currie Line, thus leaving dormant the possible prejudices of people who still think, in the light of unhappy experience, that developers are a bad thing.

"Along with the application went a letter from the secretaries of the three amenity bodies: 'We feel that cooperation between the prospective developers and the amenity societies has so far progressed along model lines', said the last paragraph, 'We welcome the developers' assurance that they will continue consultations with us, and we hope that this case will become a good precedent for the future.' Taking up this point, the Scottish Civic Trust have described the Trinity Cottage affair as a model approach for amenity groups....Linacre is not beyond admitting that some of the criticisms of the amenity bodies were very valuable. 'A number of items I welcomed and many of their objections were not objections at all. We won through because we realized that planning can take people into account and because we kept promises."

The Scottish Civic Trust's annual report also analyzed the case, concluding:

"Mr V T Linacre, a director of City Wall Properties (Scotland) Ltd., has expressed the opinion that at Trinity Cottage the work of the Societies formed a valuable bridge between the Corporation and themselves.

"Briefly, the model approach jointly agreed and tested by the Societies may be summarized as follows:

1.1 Identification of the roles of the various participants

1.2 Definition of the role of amenity societies in relation to particular.... proposals, for which there is virtually no provision at present

1.3 Formation of a group of societies.... interested in a specific project

1.4 Establishment of links with representatives of outside bodies who may wish to be kept informed

2.1 Preparation by the joint groups of a written statement of their own objectives, with their order of priorities, as a basis for negotiations

2.2 Obtaining of information and sharing of resources, skills and experience within the group

2.3 Resistance..... to the temptation to design or redesign the project

[2.4] 2.5 Recognition of the principle of social cost and social benefit

2.6 Refusal to be over-concerned at the most important stage, submission for planning permission in principle, with details of building forms, finishes and incidental matters.

2.7 Willingness to say yes as well as no.

[3.1] 3.2 Recognition of short-term and log-term planning aspects of schemes, inside and outside their boundaries, and the significance of changes

4.1 Careful use of publicity, avoiding sensational headlines and possible misrepresentations

4.2 Promotion of ... cooperation and participation as a positive and constructive process

4.3 Declaration that a model approach is intended

"It is possible not only that Trinity Cottage may come to represent for the Scottish Civic Trust a useful precedent in the work of amenity societies, but also that new building and its landscaping will equal the best standards achieved in Scotland in the past."

Trinity Park was the name I had given the development. City Wall's board was unhappy about committing its principal funding source, Standard Life, to what was still considered a potentially risky project, so for a few months, while the scheme was going through the planning system, the directors and I individually tapped favourite institutions and agencies. I tackled one of the Big Four firms of agents (not Healey & Baker!) to whom I was close; they sent their appropriate partner up from London to Edinburgh and I spent the day with him on site and with our design team, but a week later he turned it down – too speculative!

Meanwhile, I was negotiating hard with the estate surveyors at the Ministry of Works (predecessor of the Property Services Agency), and quickly secured an agreement, because the space and character and programming happened to coincide perfectly with a special procurement requirement of theirs, for a letting of the whole development.

Realizing they could not afford to lose this opportunity, I enforced what was one of the first major prelettings to a government agency with 'full repairing and insuring' obligations, when the Scottish tradition of restricting the liability of public bodies as tenants to internal repairs and decorations only, leaving the landlord responsible for keeping the building 'wind and watertight', was still prevalent. Directly that lease agreement was signed, the directors were able to forward-sell the created investment as a first-class security to one of the premier bank pension funds at a price almost double our total costs. And the agent who acted for the purchaser? The very one of the Big Four who had turned it down a few months earlier!

Four 'Firsts'

So that was four 'Firsts' in my first four years with City Wall – Easterhouse, Erskine House, the New Club and Trinity Park – and there were still three more projects of some historical significance to come in my last three years with the company. But meanwhile, I had been busy, too, with small schemes to produce income while we were working on the big, longer-term projects – some of which, of course, aborted after a lot of work and expense. I concentrated mainly on a concept which pioneered cooperation with Councils as housing authorities, whereby we designed a shopping parade where the planning authority wanted it but also combined it with provision of much-needed housing above. This created a three-storey elevation to enhance the streetscape; far better socially and architecturally than yet another isolated, miserable row of shops.

Scots law of tenure and building regulations, in relation to residential property constructed on top of leasehold commercial premises, raised two problems: (a) whether the structural slab, of which the lower surface formed the shop ceilings and the upper surface the floor of the houses, belonged to the Council as ground landlord and owner of the upper parts or to us as ground lessee and lessor of the shops, or whether ownership was divided between the parties by a notional boundary midway through the thickness of the slab; and (b) how to allocate liabilities between the parties for maintenance and repair of common parts – roof, drains, water and shared external areas – and how could those allocations in turn be passed on among respective tenants. Great fun which, unsurprisingly, did not appeal to any other developers! Special advantages, too, were that we secured the site from the local authority on a long Ground Lease at a nominal ground rent, in consideration of our bearing the total capital cost, thereby eliminating both site acquisition cost and undue delay with planning permissions. Three such schemes spring to mind.

One was at Shillinghill in Alloa, the only town of any size in Scotland's smallest county, Clackmannanshire, in central Scotland. This proved highly complex because we had to deal not only with the Burgh of Alloa as housing authority but also with the County as planning authority, based in the tiny town of Alva, requiring separate visits, only a couple of miles apart, to discuss the same project. It comprised a post office and 16 shops with 24 maisonettes above, fitting in very well with the urban landscape on a prominent corner in the centre of the town.

By the way, when Edward Heath's disastrous reorganization of local government came into effect in 1975 (just after his government lost office!), reducing great Cities to Districts in order to create monstrous Regional Councils, Clackmannanshire disappeared into leviathan of Central Scotland, whose Executive Directors, with their vast salaries and staffs and corresponding responsibilities were immediately appointed from the lowly ranks of redundant officers from the defunct local authorities. So former Clerks of ancient Burghs like Alloa and Counties like Clackmannanshire suddenly found themselves Chief Executives and Directors of Administration of enormous Regions like Central Scotland, while highly regarded Heads of Planning in much-loved towns like Haddington became impersonal Directors of Planning in detested Regions like Lothian; where they were all hopelessly out of their depths. Today, of course, buried beneath layers of government ranging from Community Councils up to the European Commission, the electorate have all but lost interest in local affairs, beyond joining occasional 'Nimby' protests.

Another was a neighbourhood centre in a large housing estate at Abbey View, Dunfermline – won by City Wall just before I joined but with all the problems ahead – eventually comprising a supermarket and 12 other shops plus 14 maisonettes above, of which 7 were designated for '5 person 4 apartment' and 7 for '4 person 3 apartment', although they looked large enough for no more than 3 and 2 persons respectively.

The third example was at Townhead in Kirkintilloch, Dunbartonshire, comprising a supermarket and 8 shops plus 22 maisonettes – 11 of them 2-apartment and 11 3-apartment, the latter on 2 floors with the former stacked alongside – apparently for a celibate community as there was barely space for childless couples. This was yet again the Burgh's first experience of mixed development, providing valuable new housing at no capital cost and bringing people back into the town centre. Only here did we get the demarcation of tenure and apportionment of repairing etc. liabilities exactly right, thanks to progressive Burgh Officers and our experience at Dunfermline and Alloa where the results were not entirely satisfactory.

I could not have persevered with these, nor with Trinity Park nor with the New Club, without a wonderful Edinburgh solicitor, Tom Hunter of Allan, Dawson, Simpson & Hampton, who owned the whole grand house at 4 Charlotte Square, which he told me they (i.e. one of the constituent parts of the firm which had grown by amalgamation) had bought in 1930 for some paltry figure. I had met 'TMH' in 1964 while with Murrayfield, when he stood in for his indisposed senior partner, David Simpson, who was company secretary to the owners of a department store on the corner of Princes Street and Hanover Street which every developer was trying to buy. I failed, of course, but TMH became a close friend and colleague, as City Wall's principal Scottish solicitor (acting on every project outside Bill Taylor's Glasgow province) throughout that halcyon era. Simpson, by the way, had become a partner in his original practice soon after qualifying, and was still pottering about the office long after I had become a regular client, continuing to do so until he died at the age of 92, by which time he had been a partner for just 70 years – surely some kind of record. TMH likewise devoted his working life to the firm, apart from his many good works, chief of which was as Treasurer to the Church of Scotland's Chaplaincy Board, for which ultimately he was appointed OBE, by which time I had moved to London. (After Simpson died and Hunter retired, the firm sold 4 Charlotte Square to its illustrious neighbour Ivory & Syme and was later absorbed by Henderson & Jackson which then took over Boyd Jamieson to become Henderson Boyd Jackson which later merged with the English firm Gateley Wareing to become HBJ Gateley Wareing, since shortened to HBJ Gateley – but my Will is still there!)

Throughout our seven years working closely together, it was always 'Mr Hunter' and 'Mr Linacre'; but when writing to congratulate him on his gong I simply had to draw a deep breath and address him as "Dear Tom", to which he instantly replied with a note headed "Dear Vivian". Professional life in Edinburgh a mere fifty years ago was uniquely formal; but social and commercial mobility, global communications and universally impertinent official familiarity, junk mail and emails have destroyed that elegant aloofness. Lawyers of my generation are the last upholders of the tradition that sent them to an English-style public school in Edinburgh, then the university to study law, then to join a firm in the city and stay there forever!

The contrast between the outlook of the haute bourgeoisie and of Labour councillors was always enlightening. I never experienced any real corruption in local government, but in the 1960s almost all councillors had a full-time job as engine drivers or milk roundsmen, devoting evenings and weekends to Council business for which they were paid bare expenses; so a little hospitality or congenial entertainment was often welcome within a trusting relationship. I never went further than once taking two honest, hard-working Labour councillors on a trip to London with a couple of colleagues, staying one night in the anonymous Regent Palace Hotel, after an evening at Ronnie Scott's Club – to which one of our guests was looking forward tremendously, especially as top of the bill was the great guitarist John Williams. Unfortunately, his friend got very drunk and, just as the applause subsided and the star was ready to play, my guest got out of his seat and, to our horror, blundered down to the front and up onto the stage, much to John Williams' bemused consternation. "What about the Rent Act, then, Jimmy?" (referring to the new 1968 Act), breathing incendiary fumes into JW's face, at which he winced but still, without losing his composure, turned to the audience and announced: "ladies and gentlemen, we have a distinguished visitor here from North of the Border who wishes to register a strong protest against the recent Rent Act. Are we all agreed that it is indeed a very bad thing?" This elicited a hilarious, raucous roar from the audience, at which Williams turned to the interloper and said: "Well done, my friend, they are solidly behind you." At which our friend clambered back to his seat, his face suffused with modest triumph. Fourteen years later, John Williams could have quelled the miners' strike single-handed.

The Wester Hailes Saga

The project which created much more publicity than any other in my life – even long before we won it – was the district centre to be developed in partnership with Edinburgh Corporation to serve the rapidly expanding SW suburbs surrounding a vast council housing estate at Wester Hailes. The architects I appointed, again, were Marshall Morison Associates, because we needed the same magic that they were displaying at Trinity Park. (Incidentally, Jim Marshall, ten years Mike Morison's senior, was a revered climber and mountaineer with several 'first traverses' to his name in the record books – the great Dougal Haston (1940-77) maintained that Jim had first taught him to climb.)

They had been struck by the revolutionary new shopping centres in Sweden, such as the Farsta and Vallingby. When viewing the submitted entries Tom Hewitson, the city's director of planning, approvingly remarked: "This lot have been to see Vallingby!"

All had been proceeding normally: we had reached the short list with three rival companies, Samuel Properties, Town & City Arndale, and Argyle Securities; all four sets of proposals were examined by the joint assessors, Blair Grosset the depute city chamberlain (today called director of finance) and Ronald Gammie, a partner in Donaldson & Sons, the city's consultant surveyors, whose final recommendation of City Wall was approved by the full Council at the end of October 1969, when the bomb fell. The story was broken by 'The Edinburgh Evening News' on 10th November 1969 with a front page story under the banner headline 'HAILES: DENIAL BY CIY WALL' opening:

"Mr Vivian Linacre, managing director of City Wall Properties (Scotland) Ltd, today denied that anyone connected with his firm had approached any councillor in Edinburgh to exert pressure over the Wester Hailes shopping development contract. City Wall were awarded the contract for the centre by the Town Council at the end of last month and Labour Councillor Peter Wilson today claimed that he received a telephone message during early consideration of the scheme asking him to support City Wall. Mr Linacre said: "No one connected in any way whatsoever with City Wall has ever had any communication at any time with Councillor Wilson." Mr Linacre said it appeared that Councillor Wilson's statements referred to something which he claimed happened last year, but pointed out that there was a council decision last December to call for an independent professional consultant to prepare an entirely fresh brief which the council approved on an entirely fresh basis. The point is that the decision has now been taken on the basis of this entirely fresh brief and an entirely new competition long after the decision to bring in independent consultants. That would take them long after the alleged approach to Councillor Wilson which I have heard of this morning.

"Asked whether he was going to get in touch with Councillor Wilson, Mr Linacre asked: "How can I? I am not allowed to speak to any councillors. I wish Councillor Wilson had got in touch with me." Mr Linacre said there was talk of a 'precipitate' decision on Wester Hailes. "In fact this has been the most protracted competition any of us has ever experienced....It is precisely these delays which have given rise to suspicions." Mr Linacre said the authorities knew about Councillor Wilson's allegations long before the final, entirely fresh round of competition was promoted and carried through.

"Councillor Wilson said he did not know what to do as a result of this telephone conversation and went to the town clerk, Mr William Borland and reported it to him. "He told me to go to the police and I saw the Chief Constable. Councillor Wilson later sent information to the Crown Office....."

'The Glasgow Herald' (11th November 1969) added:

"Councillor Wilson also stated yesterday that he had spoken to a Progressive *[the former Scottish equivalent in local government of Conservative]* councillor who had also alleged he had been 'approached' at about the same time as Councillor Wilson. Final approval of the shopping centre scheme rests with the Secretary of State for Scotland,"

'The Daily Mail' (11th November) added:

"Last night two Liberal councillors said they would back Councillor Wilson's attempts to get the Council to reopen discussion of the project. Councillor Robert Smith said that he and Councillor John Gray were concerned that the Council had decided on the scheme too quickly for the councillors to be fully briefed on all the circumstances. Mr Vivian Linacre denied that the project had been hurried through. "It was first proposed in 1965......"

'The Scottish Daily Express' (11th November) added:

"The [City Wall] contract calls for 44 shops and 4 department stores and includes a 20-bedroom hotel, a minimum of 20,000sq.ft. of office space, a filling station and parking space for 851 cars."

'The Edinburgh Evening News' (12th November) followed up under the headline 'Hailes: No Special Meeting':

"Lord Provost James McKay has turned down a request for a special meeting on Edinburgh Town Council to reconsider the Wester Hailes Shopping Centre. Councillor John Kidd said today that he had explained to the Lord Provost that he felt councillors had not had sufficient time to study the proposals in the interval between the finance committee meeting on October 27 which recommended City Wall Properties and the Council meeting (30 October) when the recommendation was approved. 'I felt it would be advisable to call a full Council meeting so that the matter could be discussed again. The Lord Provost turned down his request 'at a minute-and-a-half meeting.......I think I will be asking the Secretary of State to hold a public inquiry.' Lord Provost McKay was out of town and not available for comment.

"Scottish National Party councillors who, along with Conservatives, wanted delay in considering Wester Hailes – again because of lack of time to study the documents – are likely to hold a special group meeting."

'The Scottish Daily Express' (12th November) weighed in again, under the headline 'CLAMPDOWN':

"There was an official clampdown at Edinburgh City Chambers yesterday on the Wester Hailes affair. It came after Lord Provost James McKay interviewed Councillor Peter Wilson about allegations he had made. But after his hour-long meeting with the Lord Provost, who had called him earlier to "name the businessman", Mr Wilson said: "I have seen the Lord Provost and have no statement to make. Please don't ask me any questions about the meeting." And a spokesman for the Lord Provost said: Mr McKay has nothing to say about the meeting." On Monday night [10th] the Lord Provost said: "I am surprised that Councillor Wilson has not brought to my notice before the matter to which he referred.....In my opinion, Councillor Wilson ought, in fairness, name 'the prominent city business man' to whom he has referred."

'The Glasgow Herald' (14th November) continued:

"One of the four companies who tendered for the controversial shopping centre at Wester Hailes have asked that the whole matter be reopened. Mr Sydney Cowan, managing director of Samuel Properties, London, who were unsuccessful in obtaining the contract from Edinburgh Corporation, has written to Mr William Ross, Secretary of State for Scotland, and Mr James McKay, Lord Provost of Edinburgh, suggesting that the matter be re-examined by an independent party with no financial interest in the development. Mr Cowan says his company offered the Corporation a ground rent of £42,000 a year – more than twice the amount offered by City Wall Properties (Scotland) Ltd. who were awarded the contract – and equal participation in the equity. "We are well aware", the letter continues, "that our action in making this matter public may not commend itself to the Corporation and may damage our future relations and imperil our chances of successful development in Edinburgh. It would have been easy to remain silent, but we do feel strongly, as a public company, that the public interest must be paramount.

"Mr Norman Wylie MP, a former Conservative Solicitor-General, is also pressing the Lord Provost for 'speedy and effective' clarification of the Wester Hailes affair. City Wall plan to spend £1.5million on the development, a bigger investment than their three competitors'. Mr Linacre said yesterday when told of the move by Samuel Properties: "We would under no circumstances comment on another developer's scheme or financial tender because we are not likely to have an opportunity to study their proposals and, in any event, it would be most improper to do so." Mr Linacre dismissed the view that the City Wall development would not bring in maximum revenue for the Corporation, and pointed out that more than the ground rent figures had to be taken into consideration. "As a general observation", he said, "It is the future profitability of the development that matters at least as much as the fixed ground rent. This potential can only be guaranteed by the amount of capital that we, as developers, are prepared to invest."

'The Scotsman' (21st November) devoted a two-page spread to a feature headlined 'An ambitious risk for Edinburgh at Wester Hailes', with a preamble in bold type:

"In December 1954 James Kemp Smith bought Wester Hailes Farm for £4,750. In 1966 he sold the land to Edinburgh Corporation for £149,340, and that farm was only one of the pieces of land making up the large site on which Edinburgh plans to have a new community of 5,000 families by the early 1970s. The Wester Hailes scheme involves big money. Three weeks ago Edinburgh Corporation decided to give City Wall Properties (Scotland) Ltd the contract for the development of a £1.5 million shopping centre as a focus for the district. This decision, and the years of complex wrangling preceding it, have become subjects of fierce controversy. Now all the papers on Wester Hailes lie before the Secretary of State for Scotland." Here is the opening paragraph:

"The City Wall scheme for Edinburgh's Wester Hailes Shopping Centre, described by the city's independent assessors as a development that "could be a very exciting project", involves a novel two-storey shopping concept in which traders will pay high rents." It continues: "By plumping for the City Wall proposals Edinburgh Corporation are taking something of a risk. It could pay off. Like its rivals', the City Wall scheme is for a roofed-in, heated shopping centre; but unlike its' rivals' the City Wall plans envisage shops stacked on two levels, all facing into a central square with a 40ft high roof. In their submission to the Corporation, the development company suggested that the scale of their proposed square 'is the optimum – representing the right balance of intimacy and grandeur, of relaxation and vitality.' In their assessment of the four competing schemes, Donaldson & Sons described the City Wall proposals in these terms: 'City Wall have, by contrast, produced a very ambitious scheme....This proposal would, if successful, provide an extremely attractive facility to a wide area of population.'.... Mr Linacre said: 'The basic concept is a Civic Square, fully enclosed and air-conditioned and extending over almost half an acre, affording a spectacular arena for a variety of social and trade activities, so that the shopping centre becomes a place of public resort and entertainment. The use of levels is dictated by (a) the natural change in site contours, and (b) the creation of the necessary scale and atmosphere for the main concourse. Providing two perfectly natural ground levels with ideal access and circulation has nothing whatsoever to do with artificial 'two-tier' or double-deck' shopping. Having afforded generous car-parking and landscaping, and complete traffic segregation, and attractive grouping of the shopping centre with the office block, hotel and bus station, it was essential to exploit the natural ground levels in order to contain the shopping development around the square.....We are the only development company who have actually completed half-a-dozen schemes in Scotland within the past two or three years. In the present difficult economic conditions, it is only the most ambitious and sophisticated schemes which will prove successful. What matters to the Corporation and traders is that we are providing the most lavish and advanced form of development – i.e. the maximum capital investment for the sake of maximum future profits for all concerned.'"

'The Scotsman' (25th November) followed with a front page story opening, under the headline, ' Mr Ross calls for full details of city's actions over Wester Hailes':

"Full details of why Edinburgh Town Council chose City Wall Properties (Scotland) Ltd. as developers for the £1.5million Wester Hailes shopping scheme were asked for yesterday by Mr William Ross, Secretary of State for Scotland. A letter to the Town Clerk, Mr William Borland, from Mr Alan Hume, Secretary of the Scottish Development Department in St. Andrew's House, states: 'In order that the Secretary of State for Scotland may consider whether his sanction should be given, he has directed me to ask you to provide full details of the Corporation's reasons for wishing to accept an offer other than the best that can reasonably be obtained.' Mr Ross has been given full documents and papers on the submissions to the Corporation by the four rival developers......He requires to give his approval to the Corporation's choice of developer and the financial arrangements involved before the contract can proceed. In their financial terms the offers from the four were different permutations of ground rent and a stake in the profits of the scheme.....The Corporation in their brief to developers stated that the selection would be made on the basis of what was "considered to be the best scheme for the site, taking into account all relevant information." Last night Mr Linacre stated: "I am delighted that the Scottish Development Department are studying every aspect of our proposals. What we have offered is precisely what was asked for in the Corporation's brief....the best scheme that will bring the greatest immediate benefit to the community as a shopping centre and greatest long-term benefit to the Corporation financially.....We are absolutely confident that our financial offer was the highest that could possibly be submitted in support of a scheme which complies with the planning brief."

So it dragged on through the winter into spring. The suspense was agonising, the pressure intense and the rumours distressing. My morale was not helped by news from my 12 year-old son that a master at his school had introduced a lesson on civic society by remarking that it was of special interest as Nigel's father "was involved in the Wester Hailes bribery scandal". A minor reason for delay was that the authorities were going through the motions half-heartedly as a general election seemed imminent.

'The Daily Mail' (2nd April 1970) reported, under the headline, "£1.5m. deal starts probe by Minister":

The Scottish Secretary as asked a city council for further information on why a £1.5million shopping development contract was accepted when it did not offer the highest rent. Edinburgh Corporation wrote to the Secretary, Mr William Ross, to explain why they accepted City Wall Properties' tender for the scheme at Wester Hailes. But yesterday a Scottish Office spokesman said: 'Their explanation was not satisfactory. So the Corporation were told to give the Secretary of State more details.' Last night Councillor James Slack, Convener of the Council's Finance Sub-Committee, said: "Since then, we have had meetings with him to explain why we chose City Wall's tender.' Now the company has been asked by the Corporation to submit more attractive ground rent and profit proposals, to ensure their tender will be approved by the Scottish Secretary. Mr Linacre, managing director of City Wall Properties, said last night: "We are making a full reappraisal of our previous proposals, trying wherever possible to effect economies. We are confident that our fresh proposals will meet the Corporation's request."

'The Daily Mail' (7th April) followed it up:

"A development firm has passed on economies of several thousand pounds to a city council to help the council to get permission for the go-ahead of a £1,500,000 scheme. City Wall Properties offered £20,000 rent on a shopping centre they want to build in the Wester Hailes area. Another firm offered £42,000. But the council accepted City Wall's offer. Yesterday, Mr Vivian Linacre, managing director of City Wall in Scotland, said: "To assist the Corporation in obtaining the Secretary's consent we have adjusted our financial proposals to the Corporation's benefit by making minor savings in our original development costs. Our original estimates were, sensibly, on the safe side."

The General Election was held on 18th June 1970, Conservative Heath replaced Labour Wilson and Gordon Campbell replaced William Ross. The enmity between the Scottish Office and Edinburgh Town Council abated, and Wester Hailes regained momentum. 'The Scotsman' (25th July) reported:

"Edinburgh Corporation finance committee yesterday approved City Wall Properties (Scotland) Ltd. as developers of the Wester Hailes shopping centre which has been the subject of a bitter two-year wrangle over the selection of a company. It is understood that although the offers submitted had been revised – after concern expressed by the former Secretary of State for Scotland last year – the ground rent offered by City Wall is still lower than that of their competitors Samuel Properties of London. The committee, which met in private and did not issue later, are believed to favour the type of development proposed by City Wall, and feel that the long-term profitability to the Corporation because of the equity participation involved would be greater.

"Councillor James Slack, who chaired the meeting, and the city treasurer, Mr Thomas Morgan, would make no comment afterwards. Just over one third of the full finance committee membership was present. Their recommendation will now come before the Town Council next Thursday. It will be up to the council to decide whether the matter is debated in private again, but there is likely to be a strong move to air the issue in public.

"If the recommendation is approved by the council, it will end one of the most protracted and most complex property negotiations ever experienced in Scotland. The centre's completion date, once the official go-ahead is given, is unlikely to be before the autumn of 1972 – seven years after the housing committee initially remitted proposals for a shopping committee to a joint sub-committee. Mr Vivian Linacre, director of City Wall, said last night that if the decision was ratified......his company would embark on a crash programme. City Wall's £1.5million development has been criticised because it involves a novel two-tier concept, but Mr Linacre said the term two-tier was a misnomer. The scheme would make use of the natural contours of the site, accepting existing ground levels. The upper shopping level would have direct ground-level access.

"The committee yesterday had before them a letter from Samuel Properties declaring that it was incomprehensible, in view of their ground rent offers, that a decision in favour of their competitors was going to be made for a third time. Mr L M Roberts, an executive director of the company, yesterday repeated his call for a public inquiry. He said, "I cannot understand why decisions like this are taken behind closed doors. Too much has been swept under the carpet and it is time that the doors were opened to let the people see what the schemes actually are. Three times we have offered the best rent and three times it has been turned down." Mr Roberts said a great deal of time and money had been spent in submitting four different schemes and it was unlikely that they and some other London developers would take the trouble of submitting any future schemes to Edinburgh Corporation. It is understood that if the council approve the recommendation they will advise the Secretary of State and seek his permission for the scheme to go ahead."

But it still rumbled on Incidentally, it was infuriating that the press and even some councillors referred throughout to the figure of £1.5million simply as a label attached to the project with no notion of what it meant: whether it was the estimated total development cost, i.e. the amount to be invested, which it indeed was; or the estimated value of the created investment upon completion of the development and once fully let; or – as many journalists and even some councillors actually imagined – the sum that we were offering to pay the council! Such confusion and ignorance continues today, because politicians and the media can never admit to ignorance and everybody is a self-appointed expert on property development. Also, by the way, it is striking that only forty years ago a local authority was always referred to as a 'Corporation' – a term we never use today.

'The Edinburgh Evening News' (31st July 1970) reported under a front page headline, "Disquiet on Hailes puzzles City Wall":

"Mr Vivian Linacre.......said today he could not understand why there was still "disquiet and concern" over the decision. He was commenting on a letter sent by the Conservative group on the council to the Secretary of State for Scotland, asking him to institute a public inquiry into the two-year deliberations by the council on the selection of a developer. The council yesterday accepted City Wall's bid by 38 votes to 17. "Today Councillor Brian Meek, chairman of the Conservative group, said: "We want the Secretary of State to institute a public inquiry and we have told him we would welcome his intervention."

(It should be explained that this was during the phony civil war between the fledgling 'Conservative' group which, under the new UK Tory government, led the national party's bitterly resented incursion into Scottish local government for the first time, and the ruling 'Progressive' party which had always represented Conservatives and Unionists hitherto. Brian Meek, a celebrated sports journalist, was making mischief!)

"Mr Linacre said: "If all the Corporation's officials and the consultants prefer our scheme, then I cannot understand what is allegedly causing disquiet and concern. The Corporation's prime objective is to choose the best scheme, representing the best value for money in the long term and one that will be the greatest attraction to the shopping public. It is the scale and quality of the initial capital investment, which governs the future profit sharing, that is of greatest importance to the Corporation. If we are prepared to spend almost £1,500,000 in order to provide the most attractive and advanced form of development, then of course we are ensuring future prosperity in the scheme ......" Mr Leslie Robert said the projected costs for the Samuel scheme were just under £1 million."

Finally, 'The Scotsman' (12th August) reported:

"Mr Vivian Linacre ....hit out yesterday at criticisms of his firm's selection....His comments followed an attack by Edinburgh Corporation's decision by Samuel Properties Ltd. of London who are calling for a public inquiry into the affair. Earlier this week Mr Gordon Campbell, Secretary of State for Scotland, said he intended taking no further action in the matter, though it is understood that a decision is still to be taken regarding a public inquiry Mr Linacre, speaking from his holiday hotel in Skye *[the beloved Sligachan in the Cuillin]*, said it was meaningless to compare financial offers without reference to the merits of the respective schemes (City Wall offered a ground rent of £36,000 and a one-third stake in equity participation while Samuel's offered £42,700 in ground rent and a half stake in equity).

"He said: "Clearly, any Corporation would prefer a one-quarter share in a large amount of profit to three-quarters share in very little prospective profit. Furthermore, the basic ground rent will quickly diminish in real value to the Corporation because of inflation......The ideal from the City's point of view is the maximum capital investment by the developer combined with the best design, which has always been our objective."

"Mr Linacre criticised an editorial in 'The Scotsman' yesterday headed 'Fog over Wester Hailes'. He claimed that reference to the 'statutory hurdle of getting consent for a contract awarded to other than the lowest bidder' and accusations of the Corporation 'rejecting the lowest tender' were upside down. The fog, he said, had been artificially generated and disseminated throughout the two years in which negotiations had been going on. Technical information had been available in abundance, but had been obscured by sensationalism and distortion. "One of the latest and most sinister tricks in politics is to use willful misrepresentation and innuendo to attack authority and then to cause still further delay by calling upon the authority to investigate and dispel the confusion which the critics themselves have created." I had, of course, said 'the highest bidder' and 'the highest tender' not the lowest, but 'The Scotsman' did not know the difference. So at long last the Corporation and City Wall went ahead.

'The Evening News' reported on 24th April 1972: "A new era in shopping was begun today when the Lord Provost, Sir James McKay, unveiled a 13-ton column of stone to mark the beginning of construction work on the £1 million [!] Wester Hailes shopping centre. The centre will occupy 13 acres of land........will provide space for two superstores, 36 shops, an office block, a hotel, a filling station and parking for 750 cars. The whole area will be landscaped and will serve more than 80,000 residents. The 13-ton whinstone monolith had been extracted from Kaimes Quarry.....a "unique landmark". 'The Estates Times' quoted an immediate population of 52,000, rising to 77,000 by 1980. It described the location as ideal to serve "the whole of the Lothians to the West of Edinburgh". Two other guests at the celebratory lunch were a young pair of local Edinburgh Councillors, one Labour and the other Conservative but otherwise strangely alike: both born in 1946, both serving on the Council from 1970 to 1974 when both entered Parliament, and both future Foreign Secretaries – Robin Cook and Malcolm Rifkind! The professional team dreamed that "Thar's gold in them thar Wester Hailes" and "How the Wester Hailes was won!"

Yet the project, although so successfully completed and launched – with the hotel let to Scottish & Newcastle Breweries and the two big stores to Lipton (Allied Suppliers, the forerunner of Safeway) and the Co-op – it never had a chance of fulfilling its potential because of another example of absurd regional planning and central-local government non-coordination: the sudden expansion of Livingston New Town. Situated only 9 miles to the West, it was designated in 1962, at first little more than a collection of old mining villages, but by the mid-70s was committed to vast growth, with the Almondvale Centre at its heart, developed by Ravenseft (Land Securities) and doubled in size in the late '80s, while poor Wester Hailes sank to the level of a district centre and deteriorated rapidly before being revamped not long ago as the Wester Hailes Plaza. But what a tragedy, to have declined so young, after such an unconscionable period of gestation and with such great ambition!

The moral of this saga, apart from the need for reform of procedures for such competitions (see p.85) is that planning on a wider than local authority scale is required in order to take account of traffic proposals and to avoid conflicts between shopping centre developments such as the above – not for hierarchical regional planning that would suppress local planning altogether but simply for broader *sub-regional* planning which can integrate adjacent local plans and so strengthen them by providing context.

Linwood

Another example of commercial nemesis overtaking civic hubris – and another project that had been initiated before I joined the company but had taken years to materialize, gradually shrinking in the process – was 'Linwood Regional Shopping Centre', which absurdly retained that grandiose title long after it had sunk to the level of a mere district centre. Actually, Linwood was never more than a Western suburb of Paisley, just beyond Glasgow Airport – then known as Abbotsinch – but it had been inflated by the Rootes Group plant for manufacturing the Imp, a poor imitation of the Mini, which proved another heavily subsidized disaster. In any event, the rule of thumb is that any regional centre has shops selling fur coats and grand pianos. Like Wester Hailes, Linwood proved to be another example of the displacement of sub-regional planning by overweening municipal aspirations. A report in 'The Linwood Gazette' on 17th September 1971 told the sad tale.

"The delivery of 5,000 handbills to Linwood homes, announcing the official opening of the Regional Shopping Centre on Friday, resulted in an enormous turnout of people at this long-awaited ceremony. Mr Linacre, a director of City Wall Properties Ltd., took the chair at the opening and welcomed the Renfrewshire County Convener, Dr J McFarlane, who was to cut the tape. Dr McFarlane spoke of the reasons why the shopping centre had taken so long to complete. Although the original plans were drawn up twelve years ago, it was decided that the centre would deal with not only Linwood but the whole of the surrounding area...... As soon as the County Convener had cut the tape, he was rushed to Glasgow to attend a luncheon with the Prime Minister." After thirty years it was effectively dead and soon became a wreck. The contrast with Braehead, in this new millennium of megacentres, is absolute – such is the scale of the revolution in regional shopping within the space of that generation.

Note on Competitions

After so much dire experience of these competitions for urban centre developments promoted by local councils acting as both landowner and planning authority, I wrote articles published in 'The Estates Gazette' ("Choosing Ways of Choosing Developers") and other journals, advocating a solution to the inherent conflict between financial and design considerations which bedevilled both the prospectus (developers' brief) and assessment of the submissions. For it was impossible to reconcile the views of those, at one extreme, who, (like Samuel Properties) regarded the competition as no more than an auction of the site, solely on financial terms, and those, at the other extreme, who regarded it as a design competition to be judged on planning and architectural quality and functional merit, treating revenue criteria as the offers in the long-term; so judgement solely on financial grounds was confined to the short term. Politically and publicly, this conflict caused so much confusion and recrimination, as we have just seen, because neither the public nor the media – nor even most councillors – have much knowledge or understanding of these complexities.

So the solution I advocated, and still do, is for the council (or other authority concerned) first of all, having prepared a planning brief, to prepare also a precise statement of the financial terms required, which should be produced by the council's officials and the District Valuer and in consultation with a leading firm of specialist surveyors. It is at that preliminary stage that such a consultant is needed, not after the rival submissions have been received.

If so desired, alternative financial terms can be prescribed, allowing developers to indicate a preference, if any, but allowing no variations thereof. Thus, the price tag is fixed in advance, and there is no reason why it should not also be published, thereby eliminating any risk of misinformation or rancour and also serving the interests of transparency. Then the council is free to judge the rival proposals exclusively on their design and functional merits, with public participation. But with their predilection in favour of secrecy and control, and their inner lack of confidence to make and publicly declare such a financial judgment – "We don't know how to do it and would probably get it all wrong, so better let them do it and then we can eventually announce who (we think) has got it right" – there was never any positive response and consequently the same shambles is repeated endlessly.

East Kilbride

But the greatest competitive success that I enjoyed, thanks to a super professional team led by the genius of an architect Ian Burke and lawyer Bill Taylor, was in the competition for Phase III of East Kilbride New Town Centre. The pioneering Phase I had been undertaken by Ravenseft (when at Healey &

Baker I was the shops letting agent) with a big input from East Kilbride Development Corporation itself, and Phase II carried out by Norwich Union. East Kilbride was the exception that proved the rule because, for once, as a New Town Development Corporation (and by far the most successful of all the West of Scotland New Towns) it had a much freer hand, legally and financially, than local authorities – and more expertise among its officers. After all, its very *raison d'etre* was development, so it knew what it wanted and was determined to get it.

We were dealing with fellow-professionals, whose business was attracting investment by creating an environment to generate growth within the framework of long-term planning. In the competitive submissions, our financial offer was adequate, but our scheme design was outstanding. Ian Burke and I been to Paris and fallen in love with the revolutionary new suburban centres called 'Parly Deux' ('Parly 2', i.e. 'Little Paris') which opened in November 1969, causing a sensation throughout our industry, and later 'Velizy 2' – and still later, farther afield, 'Madrid Dos', etc. Apart from Trinity Park, Phase III of East Kilbride Town Centre was the one competition that I was able to win very largely on sheer quality and efficiency of design.

When Bill Taylor and I walked into the Corporation's boardroom for the final interview, he whispered to me: "Now don't forget, Vivian, I'll do the negotiating while you look after the legal minutiae": a brilliant tactical manoeuvre to confuse the other side, which caused me irresistibly to laugh out loud, whereupon the chairman, as we took our seats, asked "Won't you share the joke?" and instead of trying to deflect the question I told him just what Bill had said, which made them all laugh – and the interview went like a dream. I devised a financial formula whereby the terms agreed with the Corporation for our Head Lease took account of the long leases at 'improved ground rents' that I had to negotiate for the three big stores – M&S, Bhs and the SCWS – and corresponding service charge provisions. The development (named 'The Plaza Centre') was inaugurated on 13th October 1971. The programme for the event states:

"2.15 Official parties arrive at Plaza marquee. The Secretary of State [Gordon Campbell] will be introduced by the Chairman to Mr V T Linacre, Director of City Wall Properties Ltd., who will then introduce the following people in the 1presence of the Chairman and the General Manager:

Mr Ian Burke, Ian Burke & Associates

Mr George Cubbage, George Cubbage & Partners

Mr W Taylor, Rosslyn Mitchell, Taylor & Ramsay

Mr G White, Director, Bovis: Fee Construction Division
Mr D H Woolf, Project Director, Bovis: Fee Construction Division
Mr G J Testa, Main Board Director: Bovis Fee Construction Division
Mr John A E H White, Estates Manager, Marks & Spencer Ltd
Mr G R Gay, Chairman, Scottish Cooperative Wholesale Society Ltd
Mr E W G C Howell, Properties Manager, SCWS Ltd
Mr E T Petter, Group Architect, City Wall Properties Ltd
Mr J Stewart, H L Waterman & Partners"

I had to stay one night in the new Bruce Hotel in East Kilbride town centre, with John White of M&S, who insisted, when I was ready for bed, on our following his strict routine whenever spending a night away from home, of touring the whole place to make sure that all the fire doors could open, which he assured me seldom failed to reveal at least one that could not. On quickly discovering two such, he rang down to the night porter to tell him to come and open the locked doors, whereupon the following dialogue ensued:

NP: "Sorry, Sir, I don't have the keys"
JW: "Then go and get them"
NP: "Sorry, Sir, I can't, the manager has them"
JW: "Then tell him to bring them"
NP: "But he's at home, Sir, and it's past midnight"
JW: "Then wake him up"
NP: "Please, Sir, I'll call him first thing in the morning"
JW: "I am about to 1call the fire brigade, who will take their axes and break the doors down"

Half an hour later, the dishevelled, disgruntled manager arrived by taxi. Such was the power of the M&S brand! Today, of course, fire regulations are far more rigorously implemented and observed.

Note on Taxation of Land

Throughout this period a legislative threat spasmodically erupted to disrupt and dislocate the commercial property market by successive schemes for taxation of notional profits from development of land, on the presumption that gains in value from the granting of planning permission belong to "the community". Hundreds of millions of pounds in parliamentary, departmental and municipal time and expense has been wasted on still-born, abortive and abandoned proposals. First there were Development Charges under the Town and Country Planning Act of 1947, of which "unexpended balances" lingered decades later; then came Betterment Levy under the Land Commission Act of 1967, with which we had just got to grips when it was replaced by Development Gains Tax under the Finance Act of 1974, which was in turn replaced by Development Land Tax under the Community Land Act of 1975 – in the depths of a property slump!

All these measures were motivated by political prejudice, demonstrating a complete misunderstanding of the economic function of property development; all were so complex as to be unintelligible to the general public and barely intelligible to most practitioners; all proved counter-productive, merely stifling the property market and – those that reached the Statute Book – failing to yield anything like enough revenue to cover their administrative costs. Yet we had to live with this danger, whether active or latent, throughout that quarter century. When Nigel Lawson, in his first budget for the first Thatcher administration, announced the extinction of DLT there was not a murmur of protest – yet even today many politicians are tempted by the false doctrine on which it and its predecessors were based.

The General Election

During that General Election campaign in late May and early June 1970, I and most of my London colleagues were 'invited to volunteer' to spend a week canvassing in support of the Chairman's wife, Sally Oppenheim (of the Sheffield Viner family) in the constituency of Gloucester, which she was fighting to gain from the incumbent Labour member Jack Diamond. City Wall's Joint MD, Arthur Berg, was in charge of the operation, mobilising us into a highly effective campaigning force. She had failed to win nomination as Conservative candidate elsewhere, owing to either anti-female or anti-semitic prejudice or both, but was adopted here because her opponent was also Jewish. (He had previously been MP for a Manchester constituency, which he always claimed to have won because the Catholics wouldn't vote for a Protestant while the Protestants wouldn't vote for a Catholic but they would all vote for a Jew.) Diamond was a formidable foe, sitting MP for Gloucester since 1957, Chief Secretary to the Treasury and a Cabinet Minister (having been Hon. Treasurer of the Fabian Society 1950-64) as well as the wealthy MD of Capital & Provincial News Theatres; but Sally was 21 years younger with massive resources. It was a terrific battle: Labour lost heavily, yet Jack Diamond was the only Cabinet Minister to fall.

We were instructed to spend nothing in the constituency, as his friends would be watching closely; so I had to fly to Birmingham, hire a car and drive to

Cheltenham, there to stay at the beautiful old coaching inn, The Plough (shamefully demolished in the '80s) and drive daily into Gloucester. Husband Henry personally paid for everything. Jack Diamond was very bitter; he allegedly complained in a speech that "My glamorous and gallant opponent was spared no expense...." but it was (as I recall) at a private function and he would not dare suggest publicly that her statutory limit on expenses had been breached.

I am digressing again, but what a distinguished pair they were! He was became Baron Diamond and died in 1997 aged 92. She was Minister of State for Trade and Consumer Affairs in Margaret Thatcher's first administration, having been Chairman of the Conservative Party in 1973-74, holding Gloucester until 1987 and becoming Baroness Oppenheim-Barnes in 1989. Her son Philip was MP for Amber Valley 1983-87, so for those four years mother and son were, uniquely, in the House together. (He had been selected as prospective candidate by one selection committee member's vote from a short list of two, the other being my son Nigel.)

Building Design

Commercial property development always results from a reconciliation (if successful) or a conflict (if not) between architectural merit and structural engineering efficiency. Architecture held the upper hand throughout the post-war period of reconstruction, traditional continuity and material shortages. But into the 1960s the introduction of 'system building' -- industrialized techniques of off-site prefabrication, mass-concrete, power tools and piling, cranage, mechanical production of working drawings – all encouraged by the insatiable ambitions of local authorities – exalted the role of structural engineers, often with spectacular and sometimes disastrous results. Several of our schemes for Murrayfield and for City Wall were concrete atrocities, oblivious to aesthetic or environmental considerations; yet in those heady times developers, architects and town planners were all proud of our innovations and prolific performance.

Public and professional reaction against such brutal excesses set in during the '74-'77 crash, leading to the 'post-modernist' 1980s-90s architectural revival which mastered engineering science for the benefit of good building design and an upsurge in civic and interior design. It also coincided with a huge public interest in habitat and ecology. Unfortunately, however, since then it is architects who are becoming afflicted with hubris, exulting in their computer-driven mastery of civil as well as structural engineering technology as well as in their own celebrity, producing a new breed of monsters.....but that is looking too far ahead.

Main Board – or Man Overboard!

On 5th April 1971 I was appointed to the main board of City Wall Properties Ltd. This was a big compliment to me and the Scottish operation but it meant removing home from Edinburgh to Sussex and transferring three sons to new schools within a different educational system – a complete upheaval and a very mixed blessing – but at the time I did not hesitate. It was very exciting and seemed my destiny -- promotion to directorship of a public company to which I had devoted the last seven years of my life and which I fondly imagined was wholly familiar to me. In the Report for the year '70-'71 the directors were listed as: H.M. Oppenheim (Chairman), Sir Ronald M. Howe (Vice-chairman), A. Bergbaum & D.H. Montague (Joint managing directors), J. Dellal, W. King, E.G. James, Sir Norman Hulbert, F.S. Jamieson, V.T. Linacre.

Only a couple of years later, 'Black Jack' Dellal became a notorious figure in the 1973-74 fringe banking crisis that lead to the last financial and property collapse. The cause then sounds dreadfully familiar to us today. Edward Heath and the then Chancellor of the Exchequer Tony Barber embarked on a cheap-money policy, hoping to strengthen British industry in preparation for entry into the Common Market. Both then and forty years later, property developers had borrowed heavily from banks in the belief that rising property values would sustain them until their investments paid off; but then it was inflationary pressures that caused interest rates to rocket and the commercial property market to collapse like a pack of cards, in contrast to the recent banking crisis which resulted in the present depression.

But Black Jack made a £58million fortune in 1972 when he adroitly sold his bank, Dalton Barton, to Keyser Ullman, the City finance house that bankrolled James Goldsmith's brilliant string of deals, but which proceeded to make the largest loss to date in UK history and had to be rescued by the Bank of England. Having him as a colleague during '71-'72 was too distracting. (But it was in 1989 that he pulled off the most amazing deal of all when, having bought the BBC's Bush House for £55m two years earlier, he sold it to Japan's Kato Kagaku for £150m). He was still running Allied Commercial Holdings until his death in October 2012 at the age of 89.

Sir Ronald Howe CVO MC (1896-1977) was another powerful personality. Appointed Deputy Commissioner of the Metropolitan Police in

1953 (renowned as "Howe of the Yard), he was also ('45-'57) British Representative on the International Criminal Police Commission. At the end of a long but highly convivial day in Edinburgh I very easily organized a police escort to the Airport and was about to leave him with only fifty yards to walk to his aircraft (security had not then been invented) when he turned to ask, "Tell me, dear boy, which one is mine?"

Sir Norman Hulbert (1903-72) was the oddest of the bunch, having already pursued a successful business career before rising in the RAF at a comparatively advanced age to the rank of Wing Commander and then serving as MP for Stockport North, yet chiefly remembered for his three divorces followed by a final marriage to Eliette von Tschirschky und Boegendorff: I could not see his value as an adornment to the Board, but he died the next year.

As at 13th November 1972 I was listed as a director of the following thirteen companies, ten of which I had never heard of: Cerwell Properties Ltd, City Wall Properties (Holdings) Ltd, City Wall Properties Ltd, City Wall Properties (Scotland) Ltd, Crema Properties Ltd, Greenbrook Properties Ltd, Holton Properties Ltd, Kemerton Properties Ltd, Langbrook Properties Ltd, Lingtree Properties Ltd, Parkville Properties Ltd, Plutarch Securities Ltd, Three Spires Investments Ltd.

But as a public company director I had lost rather than gained authority. Whereas I would previously initiate and quietly progress a new project to the stage of presentation to Edward James who would then, if he approved, monitor further progress until confident of obtaining Board approval, now I found all my activities subject to scrutiny formally every month and informally whenever either of the Joint MDs, Arthur Berg or Derek Montague, felt like summoning me to his office to enquire at a moment's notice how I was getting on with this or that, and peremptorily disparaging or even dismissing some new initiatives without even reaching Board level. Also, of course, I was now remote from my field of operations. This was supposed to have been more than compensated by my being given a broader remit in exploration of the English regions and responsibility for shop lettings for the UK but I never gained traction with the company's operations south of the border.

Rank Organisation

Worse still, City Wall was meanwhile, in the summer of '71 acquired by the Rank Organization. This was the dawn of the era of conglomerates, when construction and industrial companies could acquire established property companies for their rent-rolls while supplying them with a ready source of capital to fuel future development programmes.

Although ostensibly a main board director, I knew nothing until it was *fait accompli*. The timing was hideous, for this was only a few months after my elevation to the main board and a few weeks after I had become committed to the move south. The take-over resulted from City Wall's expansion, which necessitated raising a fresh £6m, which Standard Life were reluctant to advance because that would have effectively given them a controlling interest, which they did not want because it would have conflicted with its large holdings in the Hammerson group and in Argyle Securities, so the solution was for Standard Life to sell its entire stock in City Wall to Rank, plus enough of the Oppenheim family's holding to give Rank ownership. Thereupon City Wall became just another incompatible acquisition such as Oddenino's and Butlin's. The new letterhead for City Wall Properties Limited showed "Directors: Sir John Davis, H M Oppenheim, Joint Chairmen; A Bergbaum, D H Montague, Joint Managing Directors; G R Dowson, R W Evans, E G James, F S Jamieson, W King, V T Linacre". Why Jamieson was still there after Standard Life had sold out I never knew. A year later, R W Evans's Rank Property Developments Ltd. was bolted onto City Wall to form Rank City Wall, when effectively the old company disappeared.

I never attended a Board Meeting of that reconstituted company, so my directorship had become farcical. Instead, the six of us from Brompton Road would arrive at Rank's HQ in South Street off Park Lane, like school prefects responding to a summons from the headmaster, where we would be kept waiting for an impressive period until commanded to enter his office (not a board-room) and sit waiting again until Sir John Davis came bustling in – whereupon we didn't actually rise to our feet but felt we ought to have done. Then, having ostentatiously rearranged all the files and Minutes Books in front of him, he glared round at us as if we were an unwelcome intrusion, before finally conceding: "Ah yes, property development" – and the meeting would proceed as if he were conducting a tutorial. Afterwards, we all tottered round to the Dorchester for several stiff rounds, before I trudged off to Victoria Station and home to East Grinstead.

It became increasingly difficult to sustain City Wall's credibility in regard to future plans. On 11 July 1972, for example, I was a guest at a superb lunch – twenty-five of us seated around Disraeli's great cabinet table in the Junior Carlton Club – given by Donaldsons, chaired by Eric Rutherford Young, but what was I supposed to talk about? The eleven other partners present were: Brian E Rowse, Anthony A Taylor, Peter D McCarthy, G Roy Simmons, Peter J Stowers, Victor C Donaldson, Ronald A Gammie, John B Murphy, David R Ives, Joseph O'Connor and Angus J Lennox.

The other twelve guests were: Victor Matthews, MD of Trafalgar House Investments; David A Beety, Co. Sec. of Caledonian Airways; Howard L Ellis, Chief Estate Agent at Associated Portland Cement Manufacturers; J W Jeurgens, Chief Executive of Makro International; K C White, Partner at R Travers Morgan & Partners; Peter N Fowkes of Fowkes & Son; J A S Hepburn, MD of Laing Property Services; C H Poole, Joint MD of Ashville Properties; J M Watt, Director, John Laing Construction; Ian Nairn, Environment Editor of The Sunday Times; A I Moffat, MD of House of Fraser Group Properties and Peter L Curnock, Properties Director of Courage Ltd. It was in such distinguished, influential company that I realized, since the take-over, how little I knew of what City Wall were doing. That otherwise tense and frustrating evening was saved, however, by my having on my left hand Ian Nairn, the writer on townscape who coined the term 'Subtopia', and on my right Andrew Moffat of Fraser's, with whom I could talk about Scotland.

Coatbridge

The end came (from Main Board to 'Man Overboard!') after I had become involved in a scheme for redevelopment of the central area of Coatbridge, conducting a series of studies and meetings with the exceptionally cultured, erudite, elderly Town Clerk named Louis Runciman, one of the last in the great Victorian tradition of Town Clerks, and Nicholas Strachan of the Council's consultants Gerald Eve & Co. We were getting on famously, working out an acquisitions budget for the Burgh in order to minimize the need for a Compulsory Purchase Order and, given patience, I was confident of securing a direct nomination for City Wall Properties to undertake the whole project, which would have proved highly profitable and attractive. But I was obliged to account to the Board for all my time and expenses up there; whereupon the MDs exclaimed: "Coatbridge? It's a dump!" Which was true and, of course, precisely why we wanted to transform the town centre.

So dear HMO himself suggested that we arrange to go and have a look, as we were overdue a visit to Scotland. We arrived there, crammed uncomfortably into one big hired car, running late, in foul weather and foul-tempered, the town centre looking at its grimmest and most desolate. They all hated it. "Who's going to pay proper rents for shops here?" (That was one of the more considerate questions.) Within less than an hour, Coatbridge was off the agenda: six months work of mine was lost, along with a lot of high-level goodwill.

Back in London I protested, in vain. I wrote to Sir John Davis, but his reply simply instructed me to comply with the Board's verdict and implied that I was seeking to break my service contract. (No wonder the man married five times – once, incredibly, to the divine Dinah Sheridan! – the only wonder being that he didn't try to marry them all at once.) It was a grotesque, bathetic finale to seven highly successful and happy years. As a grisly anti-climax, the upshot was that a bright young developer from London grabbed the opportunity to apply for planning permission to redevelop part of the site as a ghastly supermarket, which the desperate Council granted; thereby destroying much of the old town centre and making the entrepreneurial novice a fortune.

What I did not know was that Arthur Berg, a joint- MD, was leaving too (I never heard why – presumably he wasn't happy after the take-over). So the announcements appeared. In *'Property Investment Review'* (February 1973): "A R Berg has resigned as managing director of City Wall Properties Ltd. (part of the Rank Organisation) to commence business on his own account as Batchfields Ltd. and another City Wall Director, V Linacre, has also resigned." And in *'The Estates Gazette'* (13 January 1973): "Vivian Linacre FSVA has resigned from the boards of City Wall Properties (Holdings) Ltd. and associated companies and has been appointed chief surveyor to Piccadilly Estates Ltd. and a director of new subsidiary companies within the group."

I was hoping that "There is a green hill far away without the City Wall"! My prospecting was helped by the many invitations I received from 1971 onwards to deliver lectures on property development at conferences: in particular, those which were part of the Practice & Management Course held each summer jointly by Edinburgh and Heriot-Watt Universities' Departments of Architecture. Students of architecture were always much more interested in property development than were students of land economy (estate management) who thought they already knew it; and conversely, I learnt much more from them. Here are the Lists of Lecturers for each of those summer schools in 1972, 73 & 74, which are well worth recording, as the renown of so many lives on: for we were all pioneers and prophets! But whereas in 1972 the mood was buoyant, in 1973 it was uncertain and in 1973 gloomy. (Note my different company on each occasion.)

<u>1972 (19-23 June)</u>

Bruce P Beckett, Chief Architect, Scottish Development Department;

Eric D Davidson, Regional Architect, SE Regional Hospital Board, Brian D Drake, Chief Quantity Surveyor SDD,

Peter W Dixon, J D Gibson & Simpson (quantity surveyors on the New Club),

F Elliott, Chief Architect, Wates Ltd. Eric W Hall, Alan Reiach, Eric Hall & Partners (architects on the New Club) George M Levack, Bursar, New Hall, Cambridge

Vivian T Linacre, Director, City Wall Properties Ltd.

George A Macnab, Alan Reiach, Eric Hall & Partners

Robert J Naismith, Sir Frank Mears & Partners

Thomas Ridley, Ove Arup & Partners (engineers on Coventry Cathedral, Sydney Opera House, etc.)

J D M Robertson, The Surveyors Collaborative

Alan F Rodger, Edin. Univ. Dept. of Architecture

N Keith Scott, Building Design Partnership

Derek L Tatnall, Fielder & Tatnall

Anthony W Winkle, J D Gibson & Simpson

1973 (18-22 June)

Eric D Davidson, Brian E Drake, Peter W Dixon, Eric W Hall, George M Levack, Vivian T Linacre (Piccadilly Estates Ltd.), George A Macnab, Robert J Naismith, Thomas Ridley, N Keith Scott – all as before – plus James Lennie, J D Gibson & Simpson and Derek Sharp, Derek Sharp Associates

1974 (1-5 July)

Eric D Davidson, Eric W Hall, James Lennie, George M Levack, Vivian T Linacre (Percy Bilton Ltd.), Robert J Naismith, Thomas Ridley, N Keith Scott, Derek Sharp, Derek Tatnall, Anthony W Winkle – all as before – plus Robert W Campbell, Director, Scottish National Federation of Building Trades Employers, B V K Cottier, Midlothian County Architect, Angus Duncan, Deputy Chief QS, SDD and A Roderick Males, Manchester Univ. Dept. of Architecture

We have all grown accustomed now to highly specialized seminars and conferences on topics of interest to relevant disciplines within the property sphere but of limited appeal to the rest; whereas the attraction of those short courses, as the lists of speakers show, was their very broad coverage, so that all the students learnt something about everything. But for all our eloquence and erudition, we totally failed to anticipate the scale of devastation and levels of inflation that were already descending upon us. On rereading, I realize that not enough has been said about trends in developers' funding methods: so a few words now about the practicalities, without going into the mechanics of debt and equity. The premier league, of course, could always issue shares or borrow directly from institutional shareholders, relying on the strength of their balance sheets, while middle-ranking developers tended to negotiate a revolving facility on a modest scale and deployable only within strict parameters. The early generations of pioneering commercial property developers – those of my own acquaintance and their contemporaries – could borrow almost whatever they wanted purely by virtue of their reputation and record, but that breed has died out and, besides, no developer today beneath the highest rank can establish that sort of relationship with a bank or fund manager.

The institutions are no longer impressed by personalities and are too wary after the ordeals of 1973-76 and since 2008 to enter into a long-term commitment by installing one of their own people as a non-executive on the board of any company outside the premier league of developers. But hardest hit are the minor divisions, particularly for financing one-off speculative projects without adequate security.

The self-employed developer – the entrepreneur who, for all his professional qualifications and solo track-record, can offer nothing more as security than the inherent potential value of the project in question – has nowhere to turn, apparently, since the traditional friendly bank managers exercising authority and discretion is extinct, leaving only the options of selling the project on, with the benefit of a planning consent and possibly a pre-letting agreement, to a larger developer or property-minded builder who has the resources, or entering into a joint venture agreement with any of them either as a junior sleeping partner or as project manager. Even a forward commitment by a fund to acquire the created investment on completion of the development, subject to fulfilment of specified aims as to budget and return, is by no means certain to secure the short-term finance, dependent on risk assessments by interested parties. A general breakdown in trust has just about broken the market.

Now, having bequeathed the interval since 1975 to my successor, I must end by trying to look ahead from the present, assuming that the market does recover sometime in the next decade. But the timing of any recovery will depend largely on whether the Eurozone collapses, with consequences for sterling, and whether inflation takes a grip of the UK economy or stagflation sets in, or gentle growth is sustained alongside monetary restraint.

Prediction is even more difficult because of another adverse trend which has arisen since the late 1970s when the market recovered from the last great property and banking crash – and which is of our own making within the commercial property sector: the growing divergence between the practising developer's perception of value and the increasingly dominant investment analyst's perception. Working practitioners – developers, surveyors, agents, retailers – need practical information that helps them perform more effectively and improve the quality of the product; which is also very much to the benefit of investors in their long-term interests.

For commercial property development, by the nature of the materials, the time-span of ownership and occupancy and – most important of all – the effects of trends in design of shopping centres, office buildings, business parks, etc. resulting from changes in demand and technology, is a very long-term business.

But because of the universal climate of fear that has arisen from the global economic turmoil and the breakdown of trust in the domestic market, proposed new development projects are now governed almost entirely by short-term considerations. Without practical experience, investment analysts and asset managers have difficulty in discerning the impact of current trends and projecting their likely effects 5/10/20 years ahead. Preoccupation with the state of play today – taking daily snapshots and immediate action to ensure that returns from their (clients') portfolios stay ahead of the game – has no bearing on a professional appraisal of a scheme that might have taken two or three years to progress through planning, building and occupation. This gulf between the property professional's long-range outlook and the sophisticated focus of today's institutions certainly makes commercial property market forecasts problematic. It does indeed appear that, coupled with the breakdown in trust at all but the most exalted levels between the real estate and financial communities, the market as a function of the national economy is indeed broken.

Therefore, to support a project's appraisal, the developer and valuation surveyor can only rely on their own assessment of the quality of design and materials against an informed awareness of medium to long-term trends in the relevant sub-sector, which will override transient judgments dictated by the increasingly frequent, politico-economic fluctuations in the market over which we have no control and to which the newly fashionable short-term appraisals are so susceptible. This chronicle may help to show where we have come from, which in turn may help to clarify the way ahead.

8 AFTERWORDS

On quitting City Wall, Piccadilly Estates Ltd. provided a bolt-hole within which to take stock for the longer term. I was still only 44, with three sons approaching university education. Besides, the Heath government was in trouble and economic storm-clouds were gathering. At those summer school courses the mood darkened dramatically from year to year. For the country was about to plunge into a sterling crisis that caused industrial and civil strife as well as a property market crash.

After Piccadilly Estates I did a stint with Percy Bilton (later swallowed by Slough Estates), trying to diversify their industrial property operations into commercial, but the climate was becoming too hostile. I was given the title of Management Executive, which never made much sense, but I still have the memo., entitling me to use the Directors' wash-room, signed by the MD, Bryn Turner-Samuels, whose momentary blessing I once earned when, in a meeting with a loud American, he was brashly asked, "Say, Bryn, are you half-Jewish?" Whereupon, inspired by sheer embarrassment, I cut in with "No, not half: 51% -- he always retains control".

My final stop-gap was appointment as first group property manager for the newly merged TrusthouseForte in the offices beside Grosvenor House, forging the two former companies' property managements into a central estates department and reporting by solo interview with the then Sir Charles Forte every week or two, as did all the other divisional heads. He introduced me to his joint M.D., Eric Hartwell who, he emphasized, was in charge of all 72 companies in the group, whereas he himself was *only* in charge of whatever involved money and people – i.e. Charles had total control while Eric had all the responsibility. These niches gave me shelter from the storm raging outside, as well as a vantage point from which to review prospects.

I shall not venture further, because any narrative beyond that mid-70s crash would be purely autobiographical, of no interest in relation to the evolution of commercial property market – the sole concern of this brief record – which, in any event, had by then fully matured.

So those twenty-five years from 1950 to 1975 covered the development of the commercial property market from its genesis to its exodus – born at the beginning of a long post-war period of ever-increasing prosperity and reaching adulthood in its first slump.

Once the market recovered in 1977, I vowed never to work for another company, so quit London to set up on my own in Edinburgh. I have since then enjoyed my share of triumphs and disasters but nothing worth writing about because, over the last thirty-five years, creativity and innovation have been stifled by ever-expanding bureaucracy, by the conservatism of institutional finance as well as by the obsolescence of our town planning regime, our antiquated system of local government finance – with particular reference to business rates – and chaotic housing legislation. I could well have concluded on that negative note.

But a more useful conclusion from my account of those early years is the realization that the commercial property necessarily evolved through three distinct functionary phases and is now on the verge of a fourth.

The primary impulse was bound to be retail development, because (a) our town and city centres needed rebuilding or modernization, (b) post-war recovery and rising prosperity (boosted by the end of rationing, by television and overseas travel) created consumer demand for household goods of higher quality and variety as well as in vastly greater quantities, (c) the planning environment was very supportive, (d) shopping development provided a ready means of investing on a comparatively large scale to create easily managed assets underwritten by the covenants of rapidly expanding first-class multiple retailers on long (typically 21 years) full-repairing and insuring leases. All this new development reinforced established central areas in the short term, but within a generation High Street retailing declined with the explosion of supermarket developments and retail warehouses out of town, encouraged by local planning authorities, with free car-parking and lower (per square foot) business rates, thereby draining the life-blood out of town centres – yet those same planning authorities wonder how to revitalize their town and city centres! Even most enclosed shopping malls within major urban centres are of diminishing economic or environmental benefit, cut off from the surrounding main streets, quickly dated and relatively inflexible in design. Obviously, the internet and home delivery are also taking their toll of traditional retailing and retail property development. But this is looking too far beyond 1975.

The second evolutionary phase was office development, owing to the phenomenal growth of service industries from the mid-1960s onwards and emergence of financial services as a distinct, major economic sector -- and rampant bureaucracy in the public sector. The vast increase in the scale of operations of financial institutions and of government at every level generated a boom in office development throughout Britain, but largely confined to the City of London and main provincial financial centres where redevelopment is continually generated and regenerated by changes in demand, improvements relating to space planning, electronic and environmental services and facilities, management provisions, etc.

To what extent concentration on one sector causes or results from a shifting in the weight of property investment finance away from another sector is always an intriguing question; particularly now, since warehousing and light industry have emerged as the third medium for commercial estate development and investment – a more sophisticated version of what were traditionally called 'sheds' – following the collapse of traditional heavy industry. But light industry is in no sense a successor to manufacturing industry as an investment medium, since the former is an established species of property investment, increasingly undertaken by developers speculatively, whereas the latter was always financed by shareholders in the industrial company concerned. So this does raise that disturbing question, to what extent the decline of traditional heavy industry was itself accelerated by the shift of investment finance away to property development as well as to the housing mortgage market.

At all events, the demarcation between offices and light industrial units disappeared altogether when they merged into the new style of Business Parks, which have done little to mitigate the economic damage resulting from the decline in manufacturing.

Now a fourth and final phase, always promising (or threatening, depending on one's point of view) but only now emerging through a thick fog of political and professional prejudice and a minefield of institutional inhibition and apprehension, is the housing sector as a potential medium for development on a proper commercial basis and long-term asset management. It is too big a subject and too embryonic (or nebulous) to elaborate or speculate upon here; but my concept of "development leasehold" was the theme of my pamphlet (with the late John Heddle MP, another Fellow of the old Incorporated Society of Valuers & Auctioneers) published by the Conservative Political Centre in my terminal year of 1975, entitled "A New Lease of Life – a Solution to Rent Control", to which the full-page leading article in the 10th January 1976 issue of 'The Estates Gazette' was devoted – and the topic of many papers of mine which have appeared at long intervals in several journals.

Our industry will eventually have to be dragged into this new residential sector. Considering that: (a) until 1914 some 90% of Britain's entire housing stock was privately rented; (b) about half the housing supply in the USA and in several European countries is commercially rented; (c) the rate of obsolescence of surviving 19th and early 20th century stocks far exceeds the rate of new building, and (d) confidence in long-term prospects for development in the other sectors outside major cities is increasingly problematic; (e) the public are already disillusioned with the discredited system whereby house building depends upon the fluctuating supply of funds to potential purchasers by banks and building societies that control the mortgage market, and (f) the present slump has driven hundreds of thousands of households into renting; why then has our industry failed to initiate any scheme for the establishment of leasehold residential development as a major market sector?

The market in short-term lettings has recently sprung up for all the wrong reasons; sheer desperation in face of unaffordability of large cash deposits required to obtain mortgages for new houses, *dis*possession (*not* "repossession"!) by lenders of defaulting mortgagors, fragmenting households and accelerated mobility in the recession. But this is no more than a palliative, intensifying the need for long-term 'development leasehold', which must become mainstream and will, incidentally, enhance the poor public image of developers and estate agents. It will also expand and refine our own expertise and – most importantly – cure the national malaise that has afflicted our society and economy for almost a century since the Great War.

A further potential benefit of leasehold housing, of immense value to urban planning and society, is that it can readily adapt to use of upper floors above retail and other frontage users, facilitating their integrated management and ending a century of disgrace created by our pernicious systems of housing tenure and planning uses, which have caused the neglect and even abandonment of acres of upper floors above prime retail premises on the main streets of our major cities, impoverishing their quality of living as well as their fabric. So a vast virginal tract of Ground Breaking awaits us there. I explored it, not only in that 1975 CPC pamphlet but also in the introductory article ('The Temporary Utopia and the Reversion to Reality') which I was commissioned to write by the *Estates Gazette* for its special Silver Jubilee number in 1977.

The first project remotely akin to my concept of 'Development Leasehold' may be about to materialize, *but only by accident!* The Olympic Games Legacy Authority has inherited the high-density Athletes Village; a huge, ready-made estate with complete vacant possession, which it is reported it intends to convert into a new community, 'London East Village', by letting these hundreds of small apartments on (probably) 3-year leases, because on conventional 6-monthly tenancies and on such a scale the continual turnover and heavy usage would create a management nightmare. Well, it's a tiny project, but it could sow a seed that should flourish and, if cultivated by institutional investors and commercial developers, would yield a great harvest.

In any event, once the commercial property industry eventually recovers, will our academic and corporate researchers and commentators analyze the causes and consequences of the two slumps we have suffered within the last forty years and report on the lessons that emerge? And will some veteran practitioner feel impelled, sometime in the 2030s or 2040s, to write a sequel, with the benefit of a long perspective as I have had here, producing an account of the market over the thirty-five years from 1975 to 2010 – from the depths of one crash to the next? And will its first chapter be entitled – to continue this alpha series – 'Adversity'?

Index

www.ingramcontent.com/pod-product-compliance
Lightning Source LLC
Chambersburg PA
CBHW071909200326
41519CB00016B/4548
9780955615023